STATE OF THE ART

ILLUSTRATION

100 YEARS AFTER

HOWARD PYLE

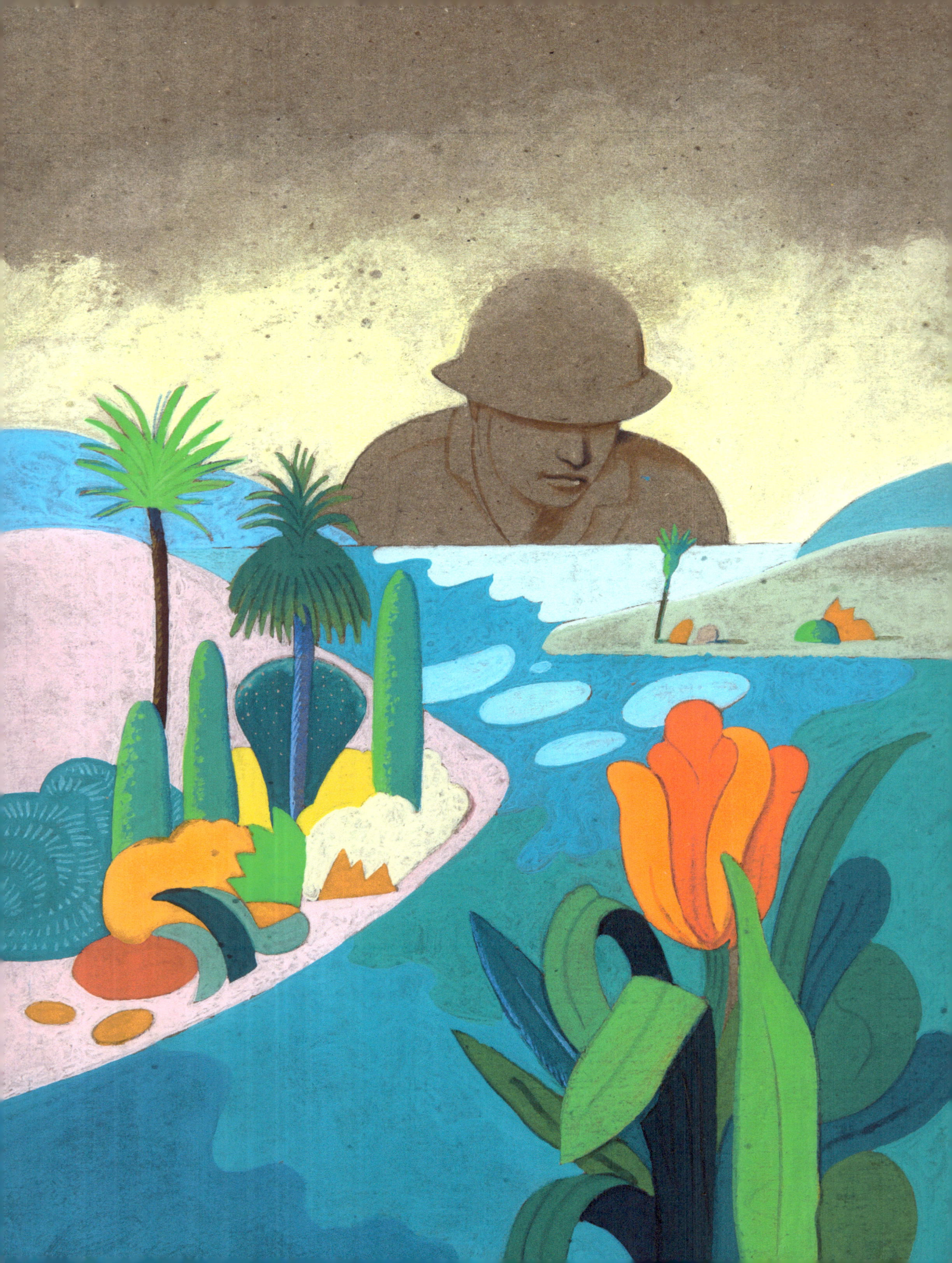

STATE OF THE ART

ILLUSTRATION
100 YEARS AFTER
HOWARD PYLE

DELAWARE ART MUSEUM
WILMINGTON

State of the Art:
Illustration 100 Years After Howard Pyle
David Apatoff

Published in conjunction with the exhibition:

State of the Art:
Illustration 100 Years After Howard Pyle
Delaware Art Museum
Wilmington, Delaware
February 9 – June 1, 2013

This exhibition is made possible, in part, by grants from the Delaware Division of the Arts, a state agency dedicated to nurturing and supporting the arts in Delaware, in partnership with the National Endowment for the Arts.

Designer: Candice Kearns

Editor: Heather Campbell Coyle

Library of Congress Control Number: 2012955850

ISBN: 9780977164486

FIRST EDITION (Second Printing)

Cover: Sterling Hundley, *Vertical Hold* (detail), 2009, for the Illustration Academy. Acrylic, gouache, and watercolor on illustration board, 20 x 12 15/16 inches. Private Collection. **Pg 2:** Milton Glaser, *Untitled,* second study for cover of *The Atlantic,* not dated. Colored inks on cardboard, 12 1/2 x 10 inches. Milton Glaser Design Study Center and Archives, School of Visual Arts. **Pg 8:** Phil Hale, *Nostromo* (detail), 2007, cover for *Nostromo,* by Joseph Conrad (London: Penguin Classics, 2007). Oil on linen, 33 x 33 1/2 inches. Private Collection, © Phil Hale 2012. **Pg 14:** John Cuneo, *Untitled* (detail), unpublished illustration for *Runner's World,* 2009. Pen, ink, copy toner, and watercolor on paper, 4 1/2 x 6 inches. Collection of the artist, © 2004–2012, John Cuneo. All Rights Reserved. **Pg 32:** Peter de Sève, *Scrat,* character study for *Ice Age* figure (Twentieth Century Fox Film Corporation, 2009). Wax pastel crayon on polyester film, 15 x 11 1/2 inches. TM & © 2012, Twentieth Century Fox Film Corporation. All Rights Reserved. **Pg 34:** Bernie Fuchs, *Oldsmobile Super 88* (detail), advertisement for Oldsmobile, 1958. Gouache on illustration board, 18 x 26 3/4 inches. Collection of Anna Lee Fuchs. **Pg 36:** Mort Drucker, *Battle for the Senate,* 1970, cover for *TIME,* October 26, 1970. Watercolor and ink on board, 24 3/4 x 18 1/8 inches. National Portrait Gallery, Smithsonian Institution; gift of *TIME* magazine. © Mort Drucker. National Portrait Gallery, Smithsonian Institution / Art Resources, NY. **Pg 38:** Ralph Eggleston, *Roughs of colorscript* for *WALL • E* (detail) (Pixar Animation Studios and Walt Disney Pictures, 2008). Digital painting, 17 x 13 3/4 inches. Artwork provided by Pixar Animation Studio. **Back Cover:** Peter de Sève, *Tailed,* cover for *The New Yorker,* January 24, 1994. Watercolor, colored pencil, and ink on paper, 14 3/4 x 11 inches. Collection of the artist.

CONTENTS

Director's Foreword   6

Danielle Rice

State of the Art: Illustration 100 Years After Howard Pyle   9

David Apatoff

Figures   35

Exhibition Checklist   39

DIRECTOR'S FOREWORD

The Delaware Art Museum was founded in 1912 to preserve the art of Howard Pyle (1853–1911), a gifted and prolific artist, author, and Wilmington native.[1] At his death, Pyle was a national celebrity mourned by people throughout the world. His pictures, stories, and teachings inspired generations of artists, including ones as far flung as Vincent Van Gogh, who avidly collected Pyle's published illustrations. The Museum launched its centennial celebration with a major retrospective dedicated to Howard Pyle, and it seemed entirely fitting to mark the celebration's end with a show that locates the value of Pyle's legacy in the world of contemporary illustration.

The scope and scale of such an endeavor was entirely daunting to the Museum's curators. Where should they even begin to select from the vast array of forms that illustration has taken since Pyle's death and how were they to judge quality from amidst such diversity? The world of contemporary illustration has large networks of passionate practitioners, supporters, and apologists but there is no single narrative that emerges. However, one voice does sound clearer and more articulate than many. David Apatoff has been producing one of the most popular and authoritative blogs on the subject of illustration since 2005. On his website, his profile reads simply, "David Apatoff really likes great pictures." This self-description belies the passion and experience behind David's expertise. While his day job keeps him busy practicing intellectual property law in a multinational law firm, David is also an artist and collector. He

supported himself through law school by drawing a comic strip named "Recipes for Fun," syndicated by the Des Moines Register & Tribune Company, and he also worked for a commercial art and photography studio in Chicago. While David has published several articles, essays, and books on contemporary illustrators, it is his online blog that has secured his reputation as one of the foremost authorities and spokespeople on contemporary illustration. For all of these reasons the Delaware Art Museum invited David Apatoff to guest-curate the exhibition, *State of the Art: Illustration 100 Years After Howard Pyle.*

As he so aptly points out in his essay: "No single exhibition could possibly do justice to the noisy, rambunctious history of illustration over the past century." David approached the task of defining trends by selecting eight individual artists who exemplify the highest quality within several different areas that characterize illustration practice today. The exhibition highlights the intersection of illustration, graphic design, and animation, presenting not an overview but rather a representative sampling of contemporary artists who have distinguished themselves by creating work of enduring aesthetic value. The exhibition also challenges some of the perceived boundaries of illustration.

A recurring theme in many of the artists' statements is the struggle to find a place for illustration in a culture that segregates "fine art" from "commercial art." As David points out, those distinctions did not always exist, as most artists before the 19th century worked "for hire" to fulfill commissions for specific patrons. And indeed, as the 21st century progresses, those distinctions—rooted in early 20th-century modernist thinking—are noticeably eroding. Certainly, Howard Pyle had no problem conceiving of himself as a great artist alongside the Old Masters. Asked about the "artistic temperament" Howard Pyle commented:

> A successful artist…is just like any other successful man—conservative, provident and normal… Titian, the Venetian, industrious and ambitious, had ministers and kings for his friends and companions. Leonardo da Vinci, whose "Last Supper," the wall painting at Milan, has made him immortal, was a brilliant architect, sculptor, engineer, scientist, and musician. Raphael, tremendously practical, was not only the architect of St. Peter's, but was an able archeologist and an authority on the antiquities of Rome. Michael Angelo wrote poetry, drew plans for splendid buildings, and was one of the most learned anatomists of his time.[2]

The Delaware Art Museum, founded by the students and patrons of Howard Pyle at a time when few challenged the value of illustration as an art form, has always given equal time to illustration and fine art. Many of the greatest American artists represented in the collection alongside Howard Pyle—Winslow Homer, John Sloan, Everett Shinn—were illustrators first, painters second. It is therefore a great pleasure and privilege to be showing the work of the artists in State of the Art. Howard Pyle would have been thrilled to find himself in their company.

I am deeply grateful to David Apatoff for agreeing to take on the monumental task of engendering this ambitious exhibition. He was ably assisted in this task by the Museum's Curator of Illustration, Mary F. Holahan.

Danielle Rice
Executive Director
Delaware Art Museum

---

1 The Museum was originally called the Wilmington Society of the Fine Arts.
2 James B. Morrow, "Howard Pyle's Pictures Grow," Washington Herald, May 2, 1909. For further discussion and a complete transcription of the article, see Ian Schoenherr, "Howard Pyle's Pictures Grow (May 2. 1909)." Howard Pyle Blog, May 2, 2011. Web. November 30, 2012. http://howardpyle.blogspot.com/2011_05_01_archive.html.

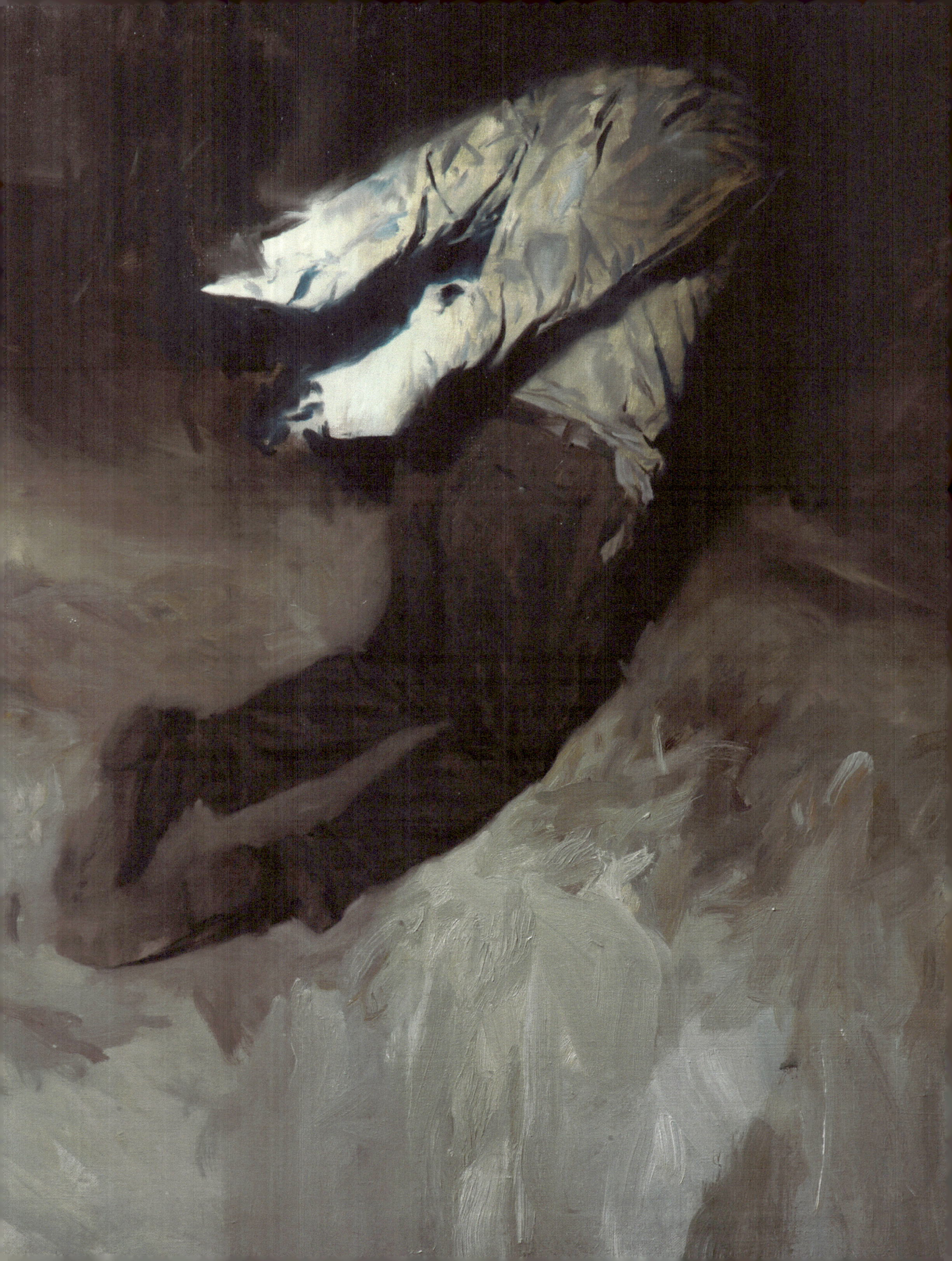

The field of illustration has changed so dramatically over the past century that it would scarcely be recognized by Howard Pyle's generation. Pictures that were once reproduced in black and white using primitive wood engravings are now reproduced digitally in full color. Pictures that once remained motionless on a page now move in 3D animation. Pictures that were once confined to books or monthly magazines now appear on websites or video games. Howard Pyle would be amazed by Photoshop and other tools used by today's illustrators, just as he would be baffled by the strange new economics of the illustration profession.

Even more significantly, the function of illustration has changed. Illustration has invaded the domain of writers. Rather than visualizing a passage from a story, a new class of intellectual designer-illustrators employs abstract graphic symbols and visual metaphors to make "conceptual" pictures. Some illustrators convey editorial content in their choice of artistic styles, including impressionism, expressionism, and abstraction. Others work in large collaborative teams to create epic works of art, such as animated films that blend pictures with story. In short, illustrators today perform a much broader array of functions than those in Howard Pyle's era.

No matter how much the face of illustration has changed, however, there remains a core set of strengths that can be traced back to Pyle, and even earlier. This exhibition focuses on those fundamental strengths and the consistent qualities of creative excellence that persist even after a century of volatile change.

No single exhibition could possibly do justice to the noisy, rambunctious history of illustration over the past century. Likewise, no exhibition can predict which young illustrators today will shape the future of the art. But a century after Howard Pyle, it makes sense to examine a cross section of master illustrators in different categories of recent illustration. The diverse talents in this exhibition demonstrate that illustration is no longer the singular profession it was in Pyle's day. But I am confident Pyle would find much to admire in the work produced today.

In the Beginning

In the past, art was the privilege of a relatively small group of wealthy patrons. Professional painters and sculptors created art for the decoration of palaces, religious sites, and public spaces. Over the last 500 years, aristocratic patrons were gradually replaced by a new commercial class, made wealthy and powerful by international trade and the birth of capitalism. These new patrons often commissioned art that was more secular, or that served commerce.

It is important to emphasize that although art patrons and subject matter changed, the quality of the artwork did not. The same talented artists who once painted chapel ceilings or the walls of the great temple at Karnak turned to the new patrons to support their careers.

One new path for artists opened with the invention of the printing press in the 15th century. Early woodblock prints of religious subjects evolved into a robust market for commercial and reproductive printmaking. Rather than selling a picture to a single wealthy patron, artists could make multiple copies of their pictures and sell them for smaller amounts to larger numbers of (less-wealthy) purchasers. By the 17th century, the reproductive process was sophisticated enough to create truly expressive copies. Rembrandt combined etching with drypoint and engraving to illustrate Biblical stories. He used a printing press in his home to make multiple copies of images such as his famous "hundred guilder print" to sell to prosperous Dutch merchants.

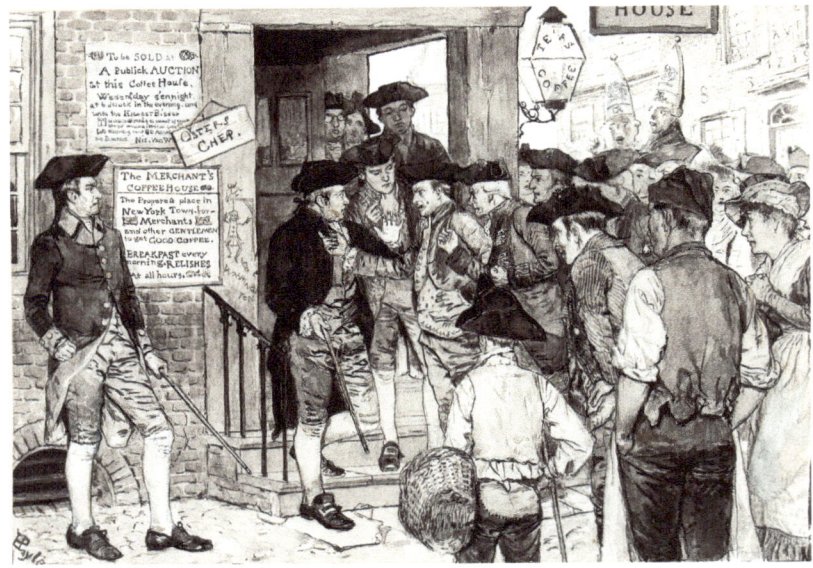

Fig. 1

The history of this technology is the history of modern illustration. There would be no modern illustration without these two innovations: the ability to create and distribute quality copies and the ability to collect small, proportional payments for that art from large audiences. This is the tradition that spawned modern illustration. Mass reproduction enabled artists and later publishers and advertisers to amortize the cost of a picture across many viewers. Each viewer contributed a small fraction of the total cost by purchasing a print, or later, a magazine, or a ticket to a movie.

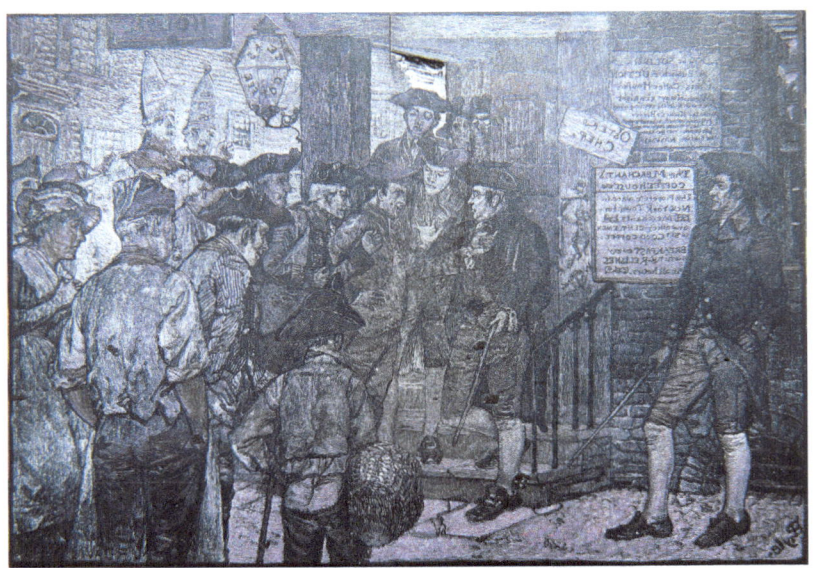

Fig. 2

The technologies for reproducing and distributing pictures continued to progress slowly from the 17th to the late 19th century. Then, the quality of reproduction took a great leap forward at the same time that the cost of reproduction dropped. Howard Pyle was a visionary who arrived on the scene as these technologies were reaching their tipping point.

Pyle began his career in an era when an illustrator's work was reproduced by a wood engraver who carved the picture into a wooden block by hand (figures 1 and 2). The engraver played such an important role that he often signed the recreated image along with the artist (figure 3).

The engraved block was then printed on inexpensive paper in black-and-white journals such as *Harper's New Monthly Magazine,* the *Century,* or *Scribner's Monthly.* Printing was key to the advance of illustration: success depended on the ability to reproduce images for mass-market audiences.

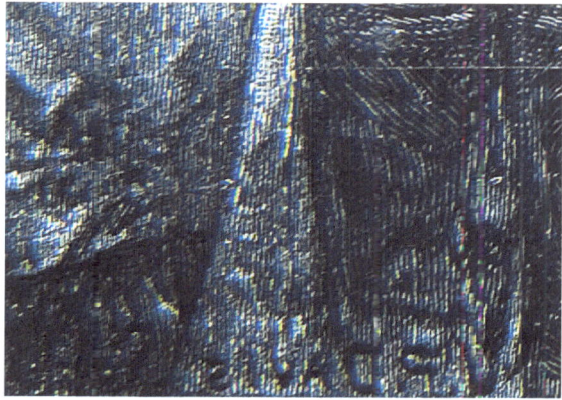

Fig. 3

In the short span of Pyle's career, printing technology improved to enable the publication of an illustration that was much more faithful to the original drawing or painting. Pyle predicted that the addition of color would increase the expressive capacity of illustration, and he urged his students to train for the inevitable day when color could be printed reliably. As Christine B. Podmaniczky, Associate Curator for N. C. Wyeth Collections at the Brandywine River Museum, noted:

> In its earliest stages, four-color printing had several drawbacks. The new process required special ink-receptive paper that could be printed on one side only; it also required exact registration of the four plates. Certain colors—greens, for example—were difficult to duplicate with yellow and blue printing inks available at the time, and heavy areas of thickly laid oil paint rarely translated well. Nevertheless, by 1903, Howard Pyle confidently instructed his students to develop their skills in color painting because cost-effective and accurate color reproduction would soon dominate the printing industry.[1]

By the turn of the 20th century, color reproduction, halftone engraving, and the distribution of deluxe magazines made illustration wildly popular. The new demand ushered in what we now call the Golden Age of Illustration.

The handful of black-and-white journals that had existed at the beginning of Pyle's career quickly blossomed into hundreds of color magazines such as *The Saturday Evening Post, Liberty, The Ladies' Home Journal, Collier's, Life, Redbook,* and *Esquire.* Magazines with large circulations and substantial

budgets created a voracious demand for pictures to illustrate fiction and articles.

Talented artists such as Pyle, N. C. Wyeth, J. C. Leyendecker, Maxfield Parrish, and Norman Rockwell employed traditional artistic skills and tools to create vivid, iconic images that gave life to fiction, historical stories, and advertisements (figure 4).

Before the development of movies, illustrators were the Cecil B. DeMilles and the Steven Spielbergs of their day, creating images that captured the public imagination and shaped public taste. They invented cultural symbols, such as the Gibson Girl, Uncle Sam (figure 5), the Arrow Collar Man, and the Flapper. They rallied the public to go to war and persuaded them to adopt a particular lifestyle or buy a particular car.

The world's largest media companies boasted in full-page ads about pictures by famous illustrators that would appear in future issues. Illustrators were richly compensated for their contribution to this important branch of the mass entertainment industry. Illustration wielded great power in the era before the public discovered that pictures could also be made to move and talk.

For the first half of the 20th century, illustrators continued to prosper by following the path established by Pyle. Styles and tastes changed over the period, but the basic business model of illustrating for books and magazines remained in place. Then, in the second half of the 20th century, the field underwent another major transformation.

The Transformation to Modern Illustration

In the 1950s, illustrated magazines began going out of business at an alarming rate. Gone were the well-funded advertising campaigns for Arrow collars and Ford automobiles. Gone were the fiction magazines that used to hold the country spellbound. Advertising revenues shifted from print media to the new invention of television. Celebrity illustrators disappeared from the scene. *The Saturday Evening Post,* which once provided the largest national forum for illustrators, finally limped out of business in 1969. Other magazines that previously purchased illustrations discovered that photographs could be more practical. By the 1970s, illustrators who had prospered under the old business model found their assignments drying up. This process accelerated with computer technology, as Photoshop enabled editors to tailor stock photographs for use in specific projects, and the internet provided new ways of distributing content.

The profession of illustration fragmented into very different disciplines. Some artists found work in smaller, more specialized markets, which presented new challenges. Commissioned to illustrate a piece for *Psychology Today,* illustrator Robert Weaver pointedly asked, "I wonder how Norman Rockwell would handle this article I have to illustrate titled, *The Psychological Complications of Being Left-Handed.*"[2] Some illustrators sold limited edition prints or game cards. Some worked as courtroom artists. They resurrected the airbrush and experimented with computers, searching for new applications for their talents.

In hindsight, this change should not have been surprising. Older artistic movements and media have been surrendering to new ones since the world began, just as one generation of technology has been rendered obsolete by the next. The Golden Age of Illustration began with the demise of the wood engraving industry, which could no longer compete with photoengraving. But as the technology of publishing images continued to improve, photoengraving in picture magazines gave way to moving pictures (just as the black-and-white movies that first eclipsed illustration would in turn yield to color movies and television).

Despite the trauma that this dislocation caused for illustrators, their image-making role lost none of its importance. It simply adapted to changing technologies,

which continued to improve and create new (although different) opportunities for talented artists. Illustrators eventually found work in interactive computer gaming, digital animation, and visual effects for live action films. The field of sequential art, including comics, comic books, and graphic novels, enjoyed a renaissance and is today a major category of illustration. Specialty magazines, web sites, and other enterprises continue to create varied opportunities for image makers, drawing on a broad range of skills.

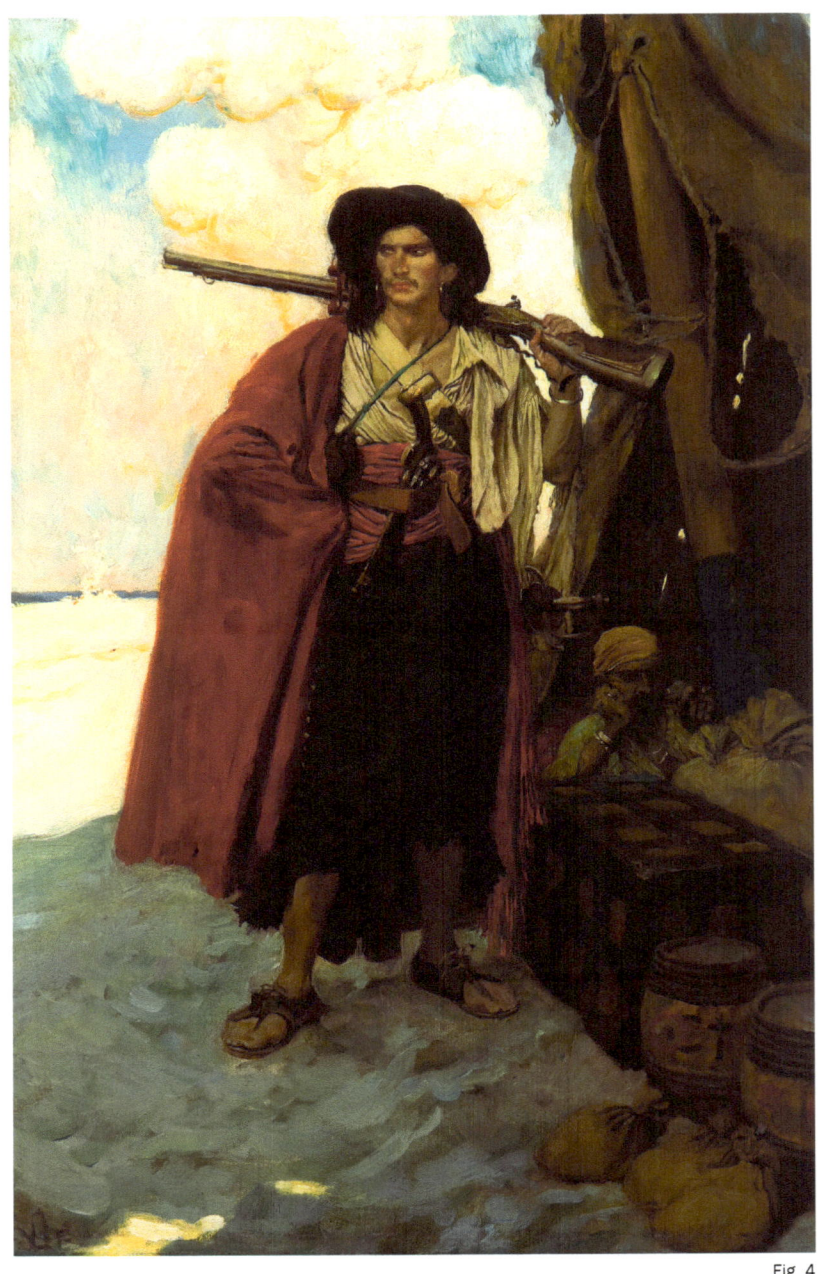

Fig. 4

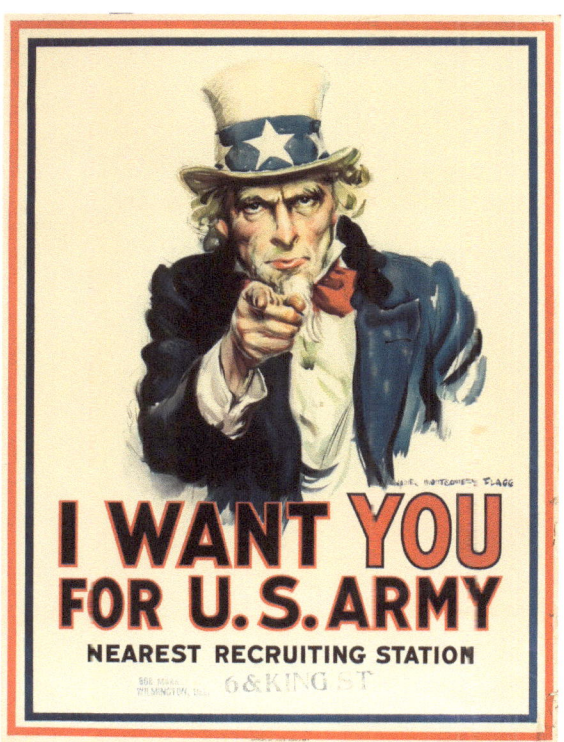

Fig. 5

The Continuing Importance of Illustration

Over the past century, illustration has grown into one of America's most significant art forms. The sheer size of its audience, its undeniable economic impact, its effect on taste and values, and even its impact on individual lives combine to make illustration a visual art form worthy of critical attention.

Throughout the 20th century, when many American towns lacked a museum or gallery to display art, average citizens were surrounded on all sides by art in the form of illustrations. By the early 1940s, *The Saturday Evening Post,* full of pictures, was selling three million copies, while its rival *Collier's* was selling nearly as many. These magazines arrived in mailboxes all across America, along with illustrated brochures from a variety of advertisers. Storybooks, billboards, and posters pressed illustrations into the field of vision, powered by the mighty engine of commerce. Today, many of the major publications of the 20th century are gone, but other platforms, such as websites and animated movies, have replaced the magazines and newspapers of an earlier era, bringing with them even larger audiences.

Most sponsors of illustration are commercially motivated, either directly or indirectly. They commission art by the most compelling artists they can find in order sell books and magazines. They hire illustrators to sell countless consumer products. Animated and live action movie studios compete intensely for the best artistic talent to sell movie tickets, just as the $70 billion gaming industry seeks out artists to make the most successful computer games. The popularity of these images, along with their economic impact, is measured every day by corporate sponsors who recognize illustration's financial value.

Illustration has also played a major role in establishing the styles, visual paradigms, and iconic images of our society. Charles Dana Gibson's famous Gibson Girl set the standard for female beauty in his era, just as John Held's Flapper shaped our image of the 1920s. The covers of *The Saturday Evening Post* served as a national bonding experience for decades, and comic book characters such as Jack Kirby's Captain America became folk heroes for American children. Later, the psychedelic pictures of Peter Max became emblematic of the 1960s. The humorous illustrations of *MAD* taught irreverence and satire to a generation of young people. Similarly, illustrations by Maurice Sendak and Dr. Seuss made an impression on American children at a formative age.

People who want to motivate others to take important actions frequently turn to illustration. James Montgomery Flagg's image of Uncle Sam declaring *I Want You* (figure 5) persuaded many citizens to risk their lives fighting in World War I. Albert Dorne's poster warning *Button Your Lip!* altered the behavior of wartime factory workers. Norman Rockwell's Four Freedoms series of posters inspired patriotism and sold war bonds. Romantic illustrations in popular women's magazines of the 20th century helped to shape not just tastes in clothing and hair styles but also notions of love, sex, marriage, and family.

In the 21st century, illustration rarely appears on the covers of national magazines. There are no more general-interest magazines with the circulation once enjoyed by *The Saturday Evening Post.* News magazines and newspapers are endangered species. But illustration and design continue to play a crucial role in our culture. In 1977, Milton Glaser's "I Love New York" logo helped create a profitable brand

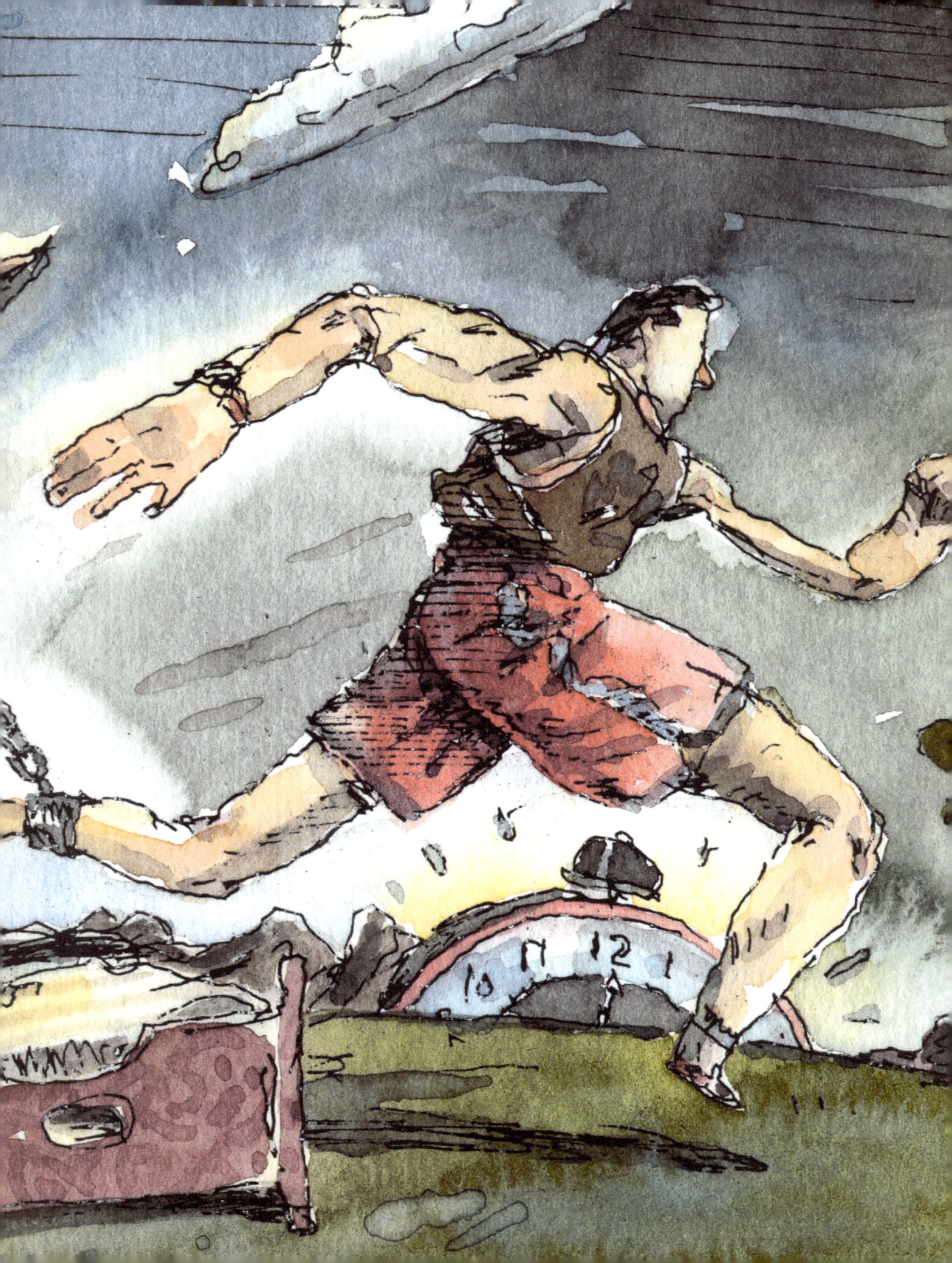

for a city of over seven million people. The same year, Apple Computer, Inc. hired Rob Janoff, an art director at the advertising and public relations firm Regis McKenna, to design the company's logo. Steve Jobs embraced the approachable "rainbow apple" that effectively represented the computer's ability to reproduce images on the monitor in color.[5] The visual imaginations of Pixar's artists have made it the most successful movie studio in the country. Illustrators today play more diverse roles, using tools and appearing in markets very different from Howard Pyle's, but they remain a significant force in modern culture.

Eight Master Illustrators

To demonstrate some of the forms that illustration takes at the end of a century of growth, *State of the Art: Illustration 100 Years After Howard Pyle* presents a cross section of works by some of today's best known illustrators. For this exhibition, I have selected eight artists who have pushed the definition of illustration in different directions.

Most of these artists are conversant with computer technologies that streamline current picture making, and which will play an increasingly significant role in the future as illustration becomes more of a digital enterprise. Software manufacturers sell dozens of filters that enable a purchaser to transform a photograph into an "illustration" with the appearance of oil paint, colored pencil, water color, pen and ink, or pencil sketches. Each of these artists has had to come to grips with the aesthetic and economic impact of such technologies on illustration. Yet, I have made a deliberate decision to avoid purely digital work in this exhibition, emphasizing instead the continued importance of traditional drawing and painting skills. Artists such as Ralph Eggleston, who work primarily in the digital arena today, learned to master traditional media first, and it is reflected in the quality of his art. Other artists who have chosen not to employ digital media have nonetheless become successful and influential in a world where illustrators have more options and face more competitive challenges than ever before. The exhibition allows viewers to contrast oil paintings, or miniature line drawings, with animated pictures to show the diversity of the illustration arts today. Today's giants of illustration have expanded the boundaries of the field since the days of Pyle.

ADVERTISING AND MAGAZINE ILLUSTRATION: BERNIE FUCHS

In the 1950s, American illustration began its great thaw from the more representational, sentimental work that had dominated the first half of the 20th century. In the words of illustrator Austin Briggs, "Floundering publications sought salvation in acquiring a new image—anything different and strident enough to retain the attention of a wavering public. These conditions produced an opportunity for the illustrator to be truly creative with a freedom from the restraints of the past never before experienced."[4]

The old ways were fast fading, and the 1960s began a period of great ferment and creativity.

No artist was closer to the center of that revolution than Bernie Fuchs. He began his career in Detroit painting photorealistic illustrations for car advertisements, but by the 1960s he was at the forefront of a wave of innovative, high energy, impressionistic illustrations that redefined the field. Works such as his portraits of the young President Kennedy and his civil rights pictures, as well as illustrations for fiction in women's magazines, caused illustration historian Walt Reed to comment in 1984

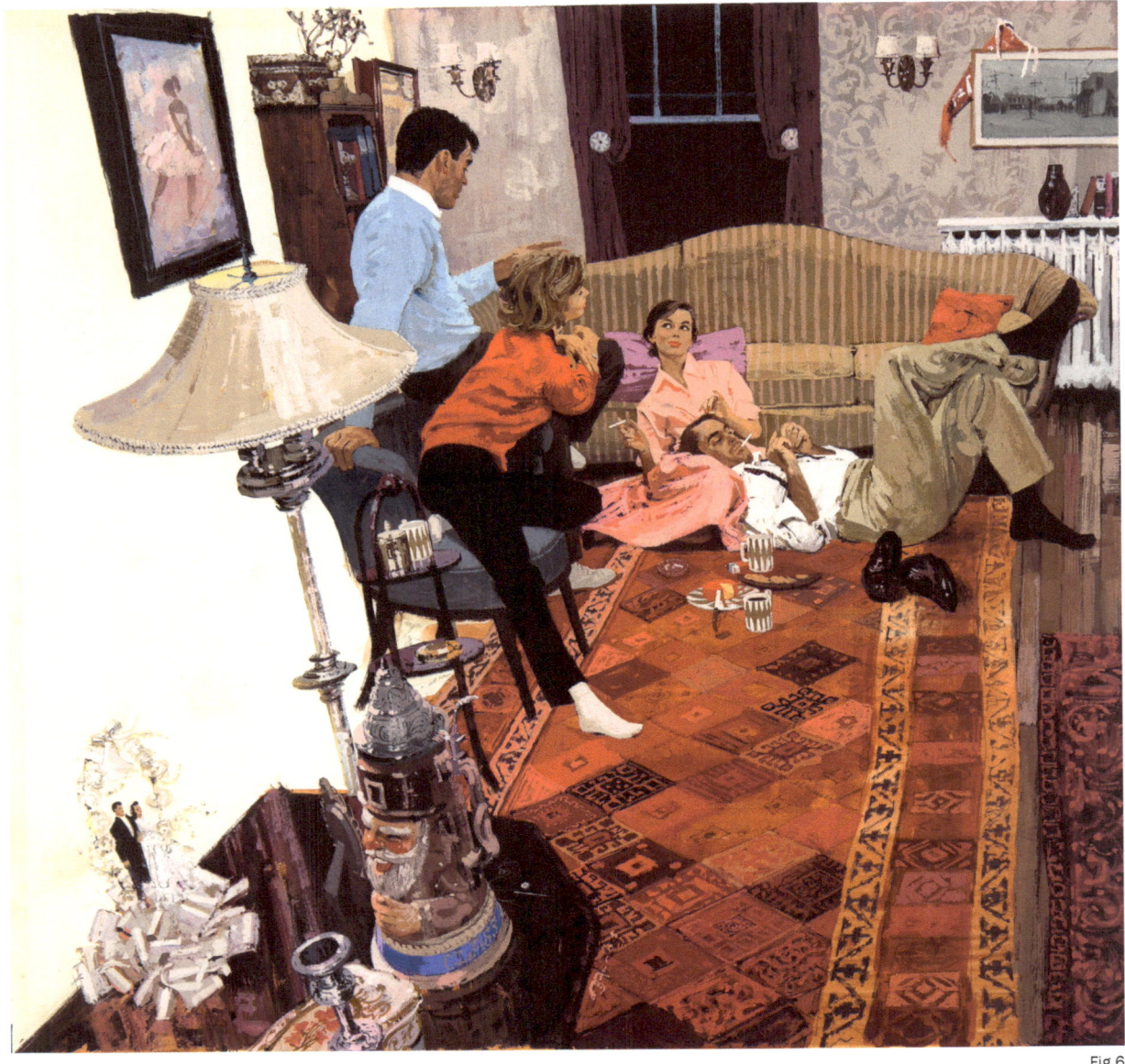

Fig.6

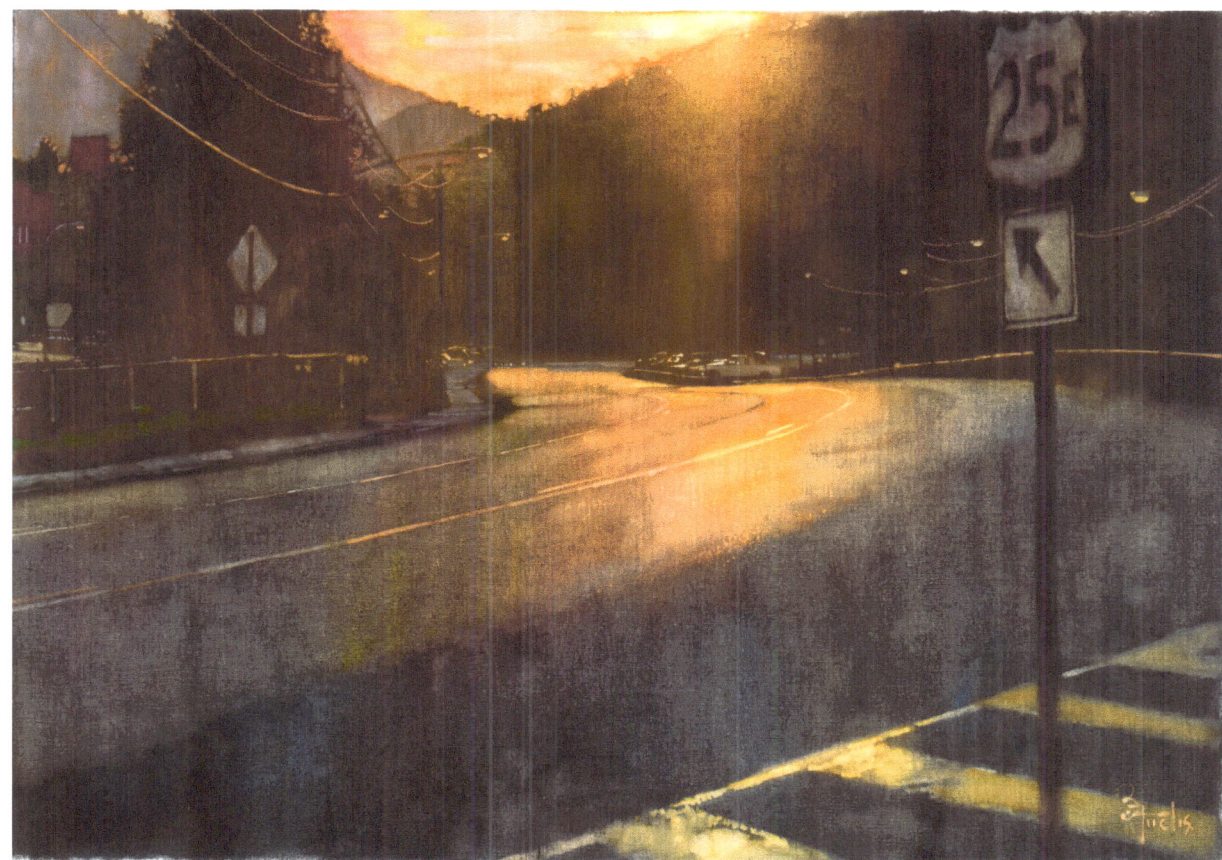

Fig. 7

that Fuchs' pictures "are probably more admired—and imitated—than those of any other current illustrator." Fuchs set forces of change in motion for the whole industry. He had a long and distinguished career and became well known around the world for his sense of color and design.

Artist's Statement

Getting the idea, that's the hard part. I try to find the thing in the story—whether it is an incident, a portrait of a character, a symbol, or whatever—that I feel is most worth translating into a picture. My aim is not merely to decorate the page but to make illustrations that will contribute to, and perhaps heighten the meaning drama, and emotion of the words. You should get personally involved with the picture.

The very first time I ever held out for something I believed in, I won. I turned in a rough for an advertisement, one I liked. The client gave it back and suggested other ideas I might try. I didn't like any of them—too corny. I didn't know what else to do with the picture and so I told them if they didn't like my version, maybe they should get another artist. Then the client called me and said, "You can do it your way." After the ad was published they had a big response to it. All of a sudden I was a hero. You give on both sides. You try to take three steps forward and only two back. In some way, you develop.

What gets you, though, is when they want you to do something like the things you did five years ago. They haven't seen what you can do or, if they have, they don't want it. That's your fight for survival. Each job you do has to be a little bit more exciting than your last. This is always in the back of your mind on every new job—to improve and experiment and be a little bit different than you were before.

—Bernie Fuchs

CONCEPTUAL DESIGN: MILTON GLASER

In the 1950s, as representational illustration was being reshaped, a whole different species of illustrator was emerging: the intellectual designer-illustrator. These artists attempted to apply a new type of understanding and visual thinking to illustration assignments and produced highly inventive and individualistic works. Led by the influential Pushpin Studios, they carved out a more symbolic and conceptual role for illustration. Milton Glaser was the leader of this movement and co-founder of Pushpin Studios in 1954. Educated at the High School of Music and Art and The Cooper Union School of Art in New York, and at the Academy of Fine Arts in Bologna, Italy, where he studied with painter Giorgio Morandi, Glaser has contributed immeasurably to international visual language for the last half century. In 1968, he co-founded *New York Magazine* and served as its design director until 1977, creating the model for numerous city magazines. In 1974, the artist established Milton Glaser, Inc. The studio's work encompasses a wide range of design disciplines, and Glaser's body of work ranges from iconic logos to complete graphic and decorative programs, as for instance for the restaurants in the World Trade Center in New York. In 1977, he designed the "I Love New York" logo, and in 1987, the World Health Organization's International AIDS symbol and poster.

Glaser was less concerned with the technical skills and polished images that had preoccupied earlier generations of illustrators, and he was not distracted by the new digital gadgetry. He wrote: "There is no instrument more direct than a pencil and paper for the expression of ideas. Everything else that interferes with that direct relationship with the eyes, the mind, the arm, and the hand causes a loss of fidelity...I like the idea that this ultimate reductive simplicity is the way to elicit the most extraordinary functions of the brain."[6]

Glaser is an influential figure in both the design and education communities. He received the 2004

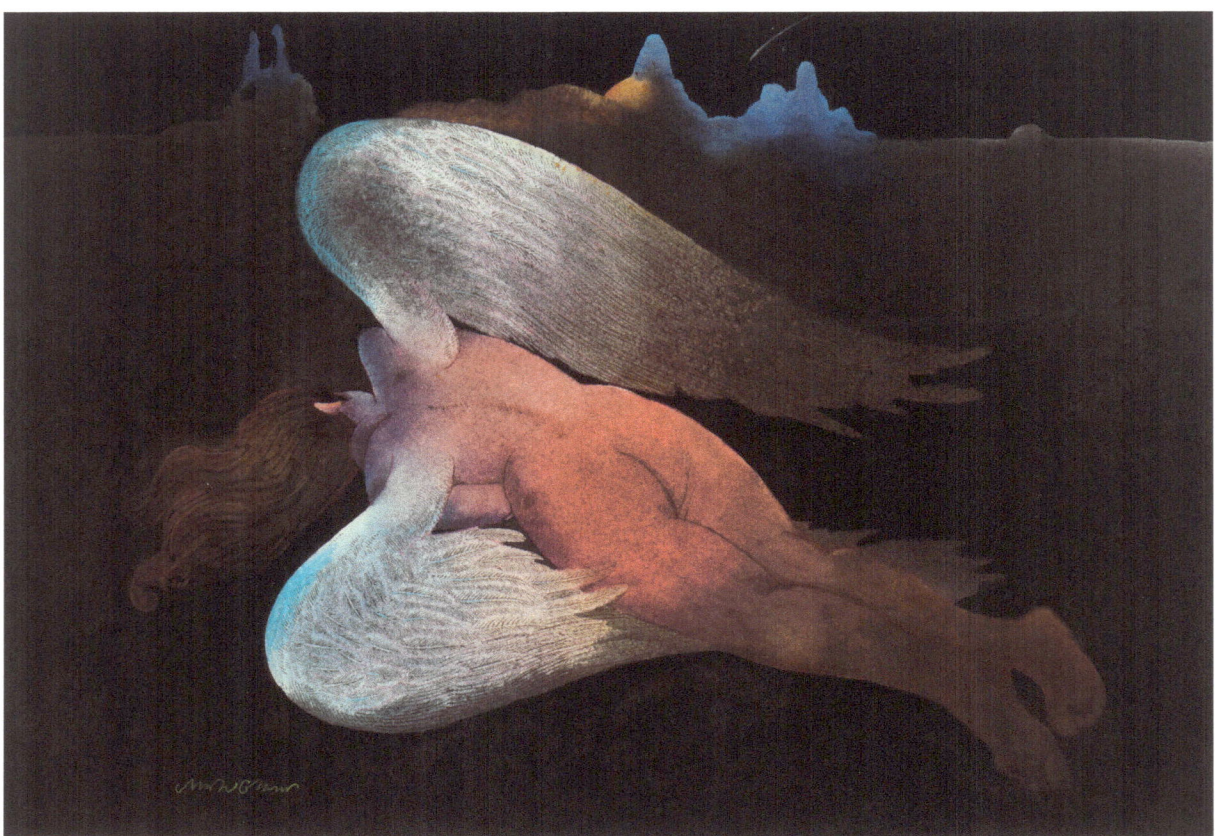

Fig. 8

Lifetime Achievement Award from Cooper-Hewitt, National Design Museum, for his contribution to the contemporary practice of design and was elected to the Hall of Fame of both the Art Director's Club and the Society of Illustrators. He has been the subject of one-man exhibitions at the Centre Georges Pompidou in Paris and The Museum of Modern Art in New York. Glaser's work is represented in the permanent collections of The Museum of Modern Art and the Cooper-Hewitt, National Design Museum, New York; Smithsonian Institution, Washington, D.C; and the Israel Museum, Jerusalem.

Artist's Statement

I'm frequently asked about the distinction between Illustration and Fine Art, and must admit that I am mystified, largely because within the context of the question, there is usually no agreement as to what art is, and certainly no agreement about what the "fine" part of Fine Art is.

As I recall, "refining" is a process where metal is heated to the point where all the impurities contained within it are vaporized and what is left behind is pure and unadulterated. Similarly, Fine Art is without adulterating elements, or, one might say, corruption. I suppose then that art can be corrupt, or is susceptible to other influences that pervert its central objective. The "What is the central objective?" is often discussed, but remains obscure.

In my own mind, Art, whether "fine" or not, has a central role in human activity and civilization, the establishment of commonality or community. Art serves as a point of agreement among humans that creates a sense of unity and shared belief. It acts almost in the same way as religion or philosophy, but without ideology. Those who share an "art" experience tend to feel something in common that transcends other forms of affiliation, and goes beyond aspects of selfishness and personal gain. Art's purpose is independent of material advantage and, ultimately, is a mechanism to help human survival through a kind of tribal identification. It is, in short, a survival mechanism to diminish the

frequency of people killing each other. When one speaks of Illustration, on the other hand, its function is indicated by the Latin word itself, "lustrāre," or "to shed light on." This may or may not fall into the category of art.

Ultimately, Art's purpose seems to be as the instrument that delivers the experience of beauty to our brains. This phenomenon can be quantified by the increase of neurological activity that occurs when it is in the presence of what we then call "Art." I'm beginning to believe that soon we will be able to measure this change in brain activity and, perhaps, finally determine whether something is Art or not beyond personal subjective opinion.

—Milton Glaser

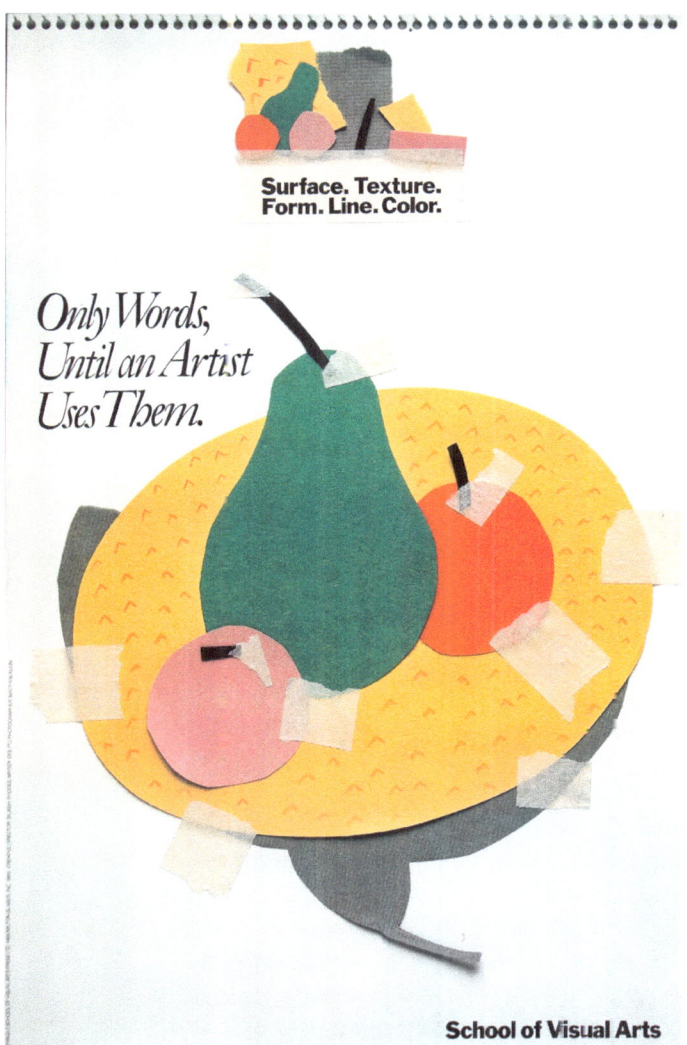

Surface. Texture. Form. Line. Color.

Only Words, Until an Artist Uses Them.

School of Visual Arts

Fig. 9

SEQUENTIAL ART: MORT DRUCKER

Toward the end of Howard Pyle's career, pen-and-ink illustrators began to find work in the new field of comic strips. Within a few decades, this sequential art form developed a huge following. Characters such as Krazy Kat, Prince Valiant, and Flash Gordon became cultural icons. Today, comic strip characters, such as Charlie Brown and Lucy from *Peanuts* and the boy and his tiger from *Calvin and Hobbes,* are internationally known and highly regarded by critics.

In the 1930s, a separate branch of sequential art—comic books—took shape and quickly gained as much economic and cultural significance as comic strips. Comic book characters such as Batman, Spiderman, and Superman went on to play a multi-billion-dollar role in the film, toy, and gaming industries. They have become the myths and legends of our society, much the way heroes such as Hercules and Achilles were for ancient societies. More recently, sequential art has matured into the form of graphic novels. Such works are now being created by Pulitzer Prize-winning artists and writers.

In the second half of the 20th century, no graphic humor magazine had a wider impact than *MAD.* Among its most famous artists was Mort Drucker, a brilliant and influential caricaturist, internationally renowned for his pen-and-ink work. Drucker is largely self-taught as an artist. He learned from studying the work of illustrators such as Robert Fawcett, Albert Dorne, and Ronald Searle, and eventually developed his own distinctive style. He began his art career as an assistant, drawing backgrounds for a syndicated comic strip, and then progressed to comic books and freelance illustrations before settling in for a long, storied tenure at *MAD,* where his movie satires soon became the centerpiece of the magazine. In the 1970s, Drucker's uncanny skill as a caricaturist was recognized by *TIME,* which commissioned him to do several covers.

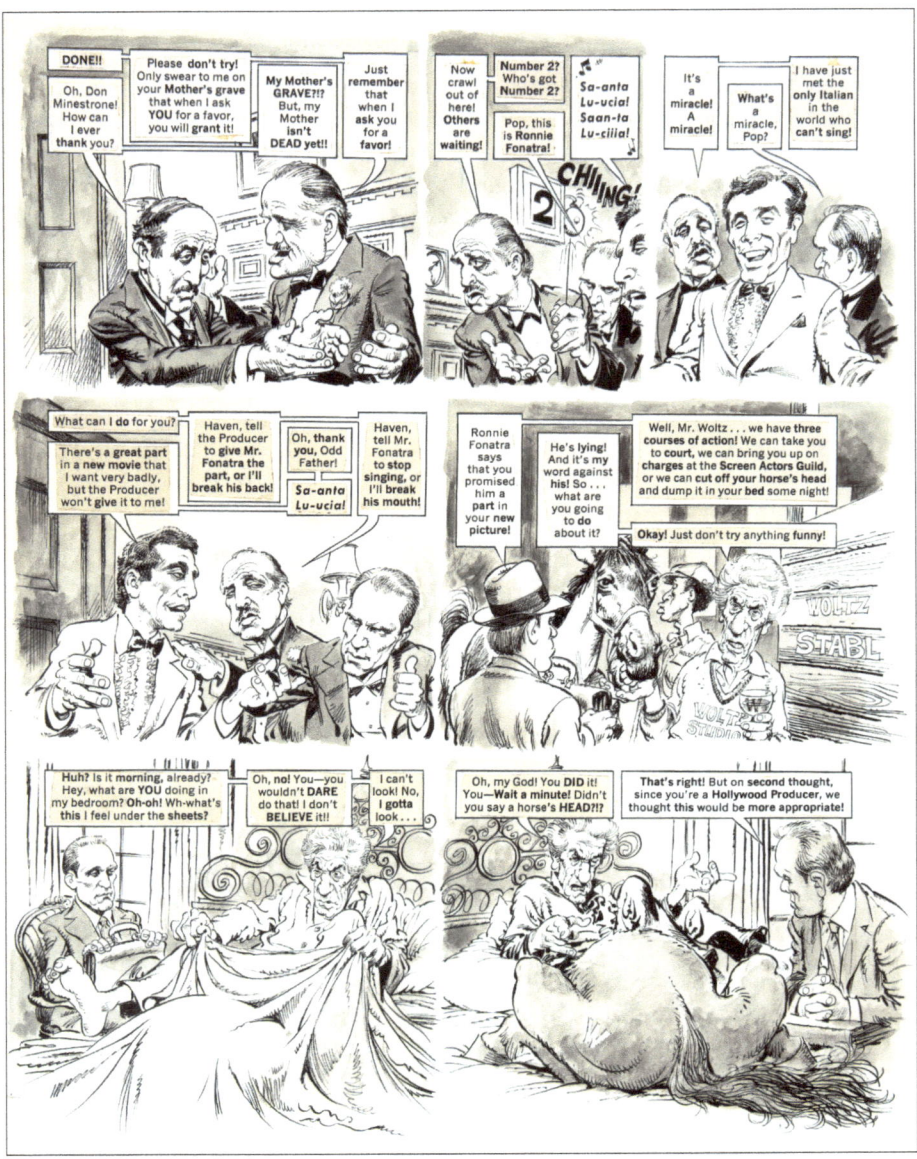

Fig. 10

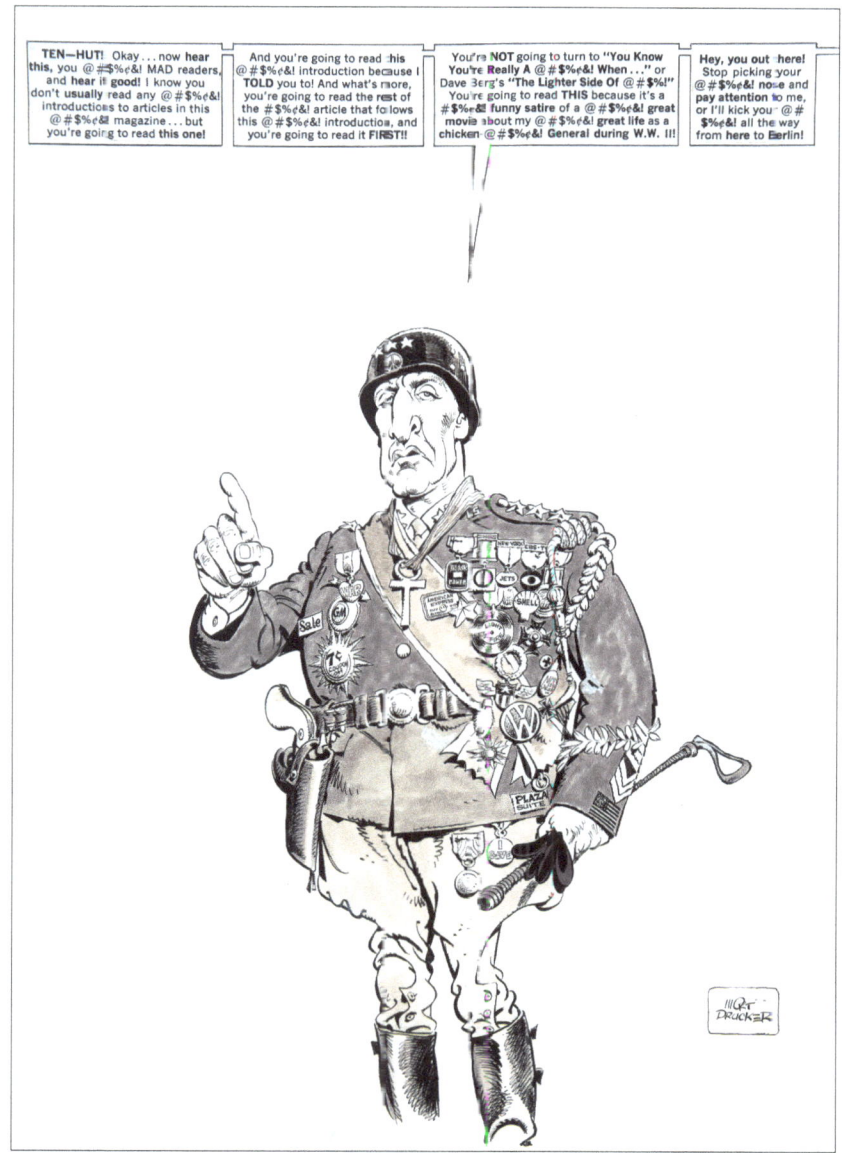

Fig. 11

Artist's Statement

My approach hasn't really changed over the course of my career. I do everything by hand, using a pencil and an ink pen or brush. I don't use a light box or a computer or other technical aids. I use photographs for research but I don't trace or copy them. Being an accurate copier doesn't insure good likenesses. You shouldn't be too influenced by your research. A caricaturist, like a portrait artist, deals not with reality but with images reduced to line and/or tone on a two-dimensional surface. I put the figure where I think it belongs and not where the photo dictates. Staging an illustration around available reference points limits your freedom to tell a story effectively. The important thing is to think through what the job requires and try to do the best I can for each particular job. I always find time to put something extra, something special in each picture. People notice it and respond to what I do, sometimes more than they respond to the main subject of the picture. That response makes the process more meaningful for me. I think about it as I draw. I face deadlines like all illustrators, but after a long career I still try to find time to make each picture unique.

—Mort Drucker

ILLUSTRATION AND PAINTING: PHIL HALE

Some illustrators simultaneously pursue careers in both the fine art world and the commercial art world, creating major paintings that are sold in art galleries as well as images that are reproduced in books and magazines. The boundaries between "fine art" and "illustration" have become increasingly porous over the years, especially as popular art becomes more culturally significant.

Born in the United States, where he studied with painter Rick Berry, Hale now resides in England. He is one of the boldest illustrators of his generation, consistently making powerful compositions that combine traditional realism with moody, complex, evocative themes. Highly regarded for his covers for the books of Joseph Conrad and Steven King,

Hale refuses to be bound by traditional commercial categories and works freely in fine and illustrative art.

Artist's Statement

My career in illustration stretched from 1981 to 2000, with a few later forays and relapses. Considering how completely my teenage years were immersed in the world of Norman Rockwell, N. C. Wyeth, Andrew Wyeth, Frank Frazetta, and the annuals of the Society of Illustrators, it was a profound shock to discover that my own internal landscape and practice was so ill-suited to the actual work of traditional illustration. Problems materialized with almost my first professional job. The solution that would most effectively and beautifully resolve the painting had nothing to do with the text. This became a source of grief and discomfort for years to come.

In some ways it was useful that this contradiction

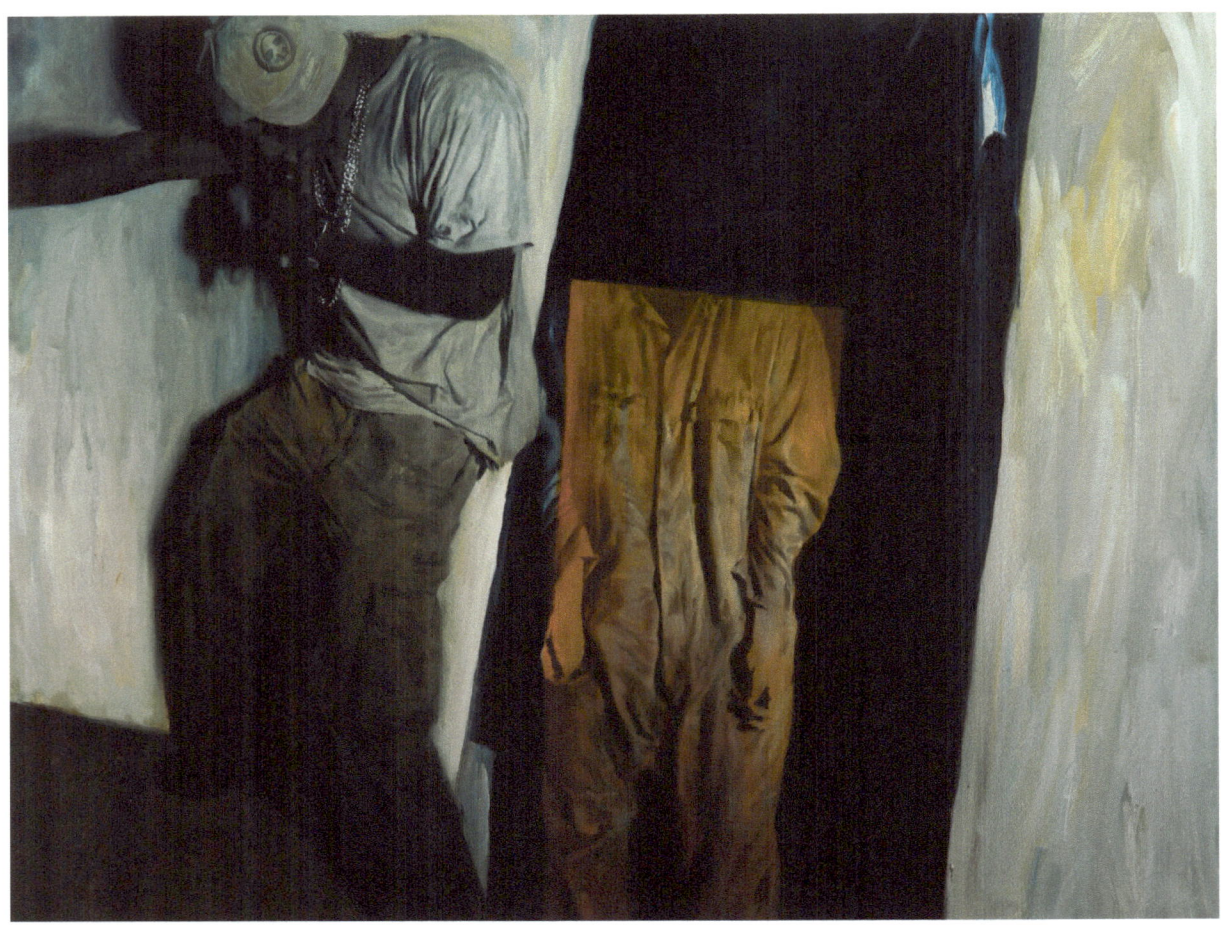

Fig. 12

forced issues to the surface. Painting has the advantage that the failure or compromise is right in front of you to be considered. My core impulse was to become a better painter, and the more illustration work I did, the more its necessary strictures and compromises became trouble. In my own work I could resolve the piece in any way I saw fit, even if it involved smearing, wiping, blurring, sanding, crushing, obscuring with black abstracted blobs, or simply stopping.

I was very involved in using the painting as a tool, not a product or some kind of necessary chair to sit on. I wanted to develop my idea of what was possible, what potential could be exploited. But my reflexive behavior

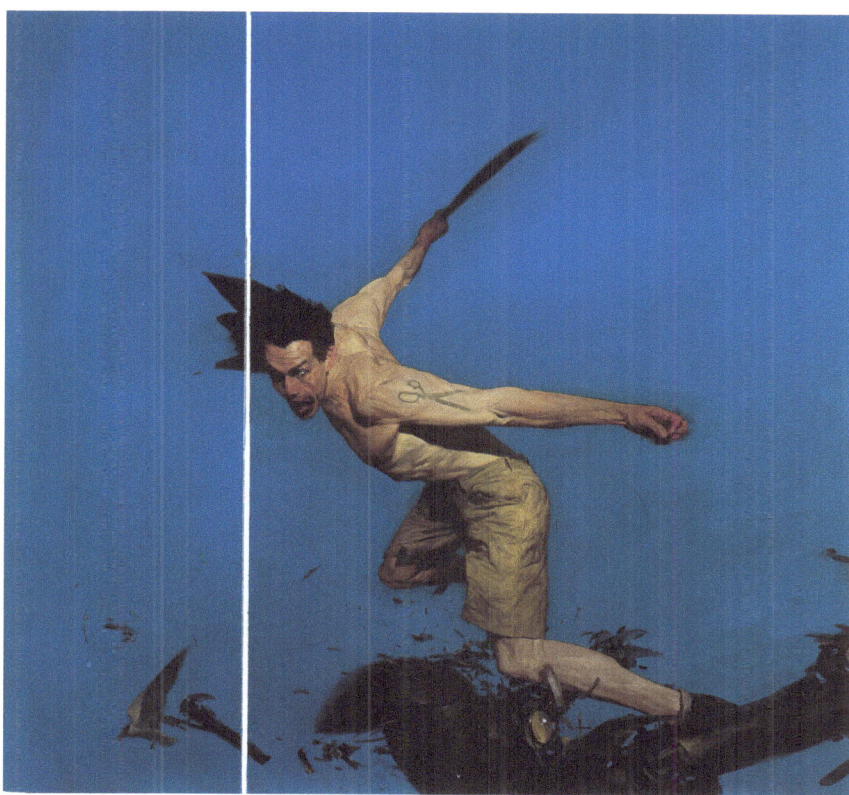

Fig. 13

under the guidelines of the illustration job had me shepherding goats into a cul-de-sac. And more: illustration often requires an initial pop impact, some kind of immediacy to engage the viewer. But what about pieces with a slow attack? Everyone has had the experience of compulsively listening to a song that initially seemed to offer nothing. Only after twenty or thirty listens does the true content become accessible.

Obviously, the artist and the viewer require very different things from a piece. If you dug up an anonymous painting in a field it would be irrelevant to the viewer whether the artist's point of attack had been practical or personal. But that is not true of the artist; folding someone else's needs into the decisions dramatically alters the feedback cycle you have with the work, a third (or fourth!) invisible force to bend the line. This has nothing to do with the value or worthiness of the piece. But it does let the artist know that the problems in front of you are yours and not something imposed upon you. And finally, it was useful for me to produce art that could fail, that could be an experiment, or an unfamiliar lever to crank open something new. The unstable and the uncertain

allowed something to happen next. Art that was too strongly and clearly constructed closed off a host of other potentials. You choose one path and everything else disappears. It is important to commit, but you can commit to ambiguity and an acceptance that much is unknowable.

The great illustrators found a way to fuse the personal and the practical in ways that I could not. There was a long and relentless climb over the centuries, an unbroken thread, that produced Pyle and N.C. Wyeth and their inheritors. But the "Command Z" button on a computer has undone a lot of that.

My unhappiness with the illustration work I was producing pushed me into portraiture and then fine art (though that is a dumb misnomer in many ways). But as I progressed, an unexpected element that is normally associated with illustration turned out to be at the center of the newer work: narrative. In a way I stayed true to my original and unselfconscious love of illustration

—Phil Hale

NARRATIVE AND CONCEPTUAL ART: STERLING HUNDLEY

Sterling Hundley is one of the major illustrators of the current generation that seamlessly combines traditional artistic media with digital technology. He built a strong following at a young age and his work has appeared in *Rolling Stone, Entertainment Weekly, The Atlantic, The New Yorker, The Progressive, Vibe, Utne Reader, The New York Times,* and *Los Angeles Times*. The winner of three gold and two silver medals from the Society of Illustrators in New York, Hundley has also been awarded gold and silver medals from the Illustrators Club in Washington, D.C. Feature articles on Hundley's work have appeared in *Communication Arts, Print, Illustration Now,* and *Step-by-Step Graphics.*

Hundley is an influential teacher and mentor for the next generation of illustrators. One of the core instructors of The Illustration Academy in Sarasota, Florida, he is also a professor in the Department of Communication Arts at Virginia Commonwealth University.

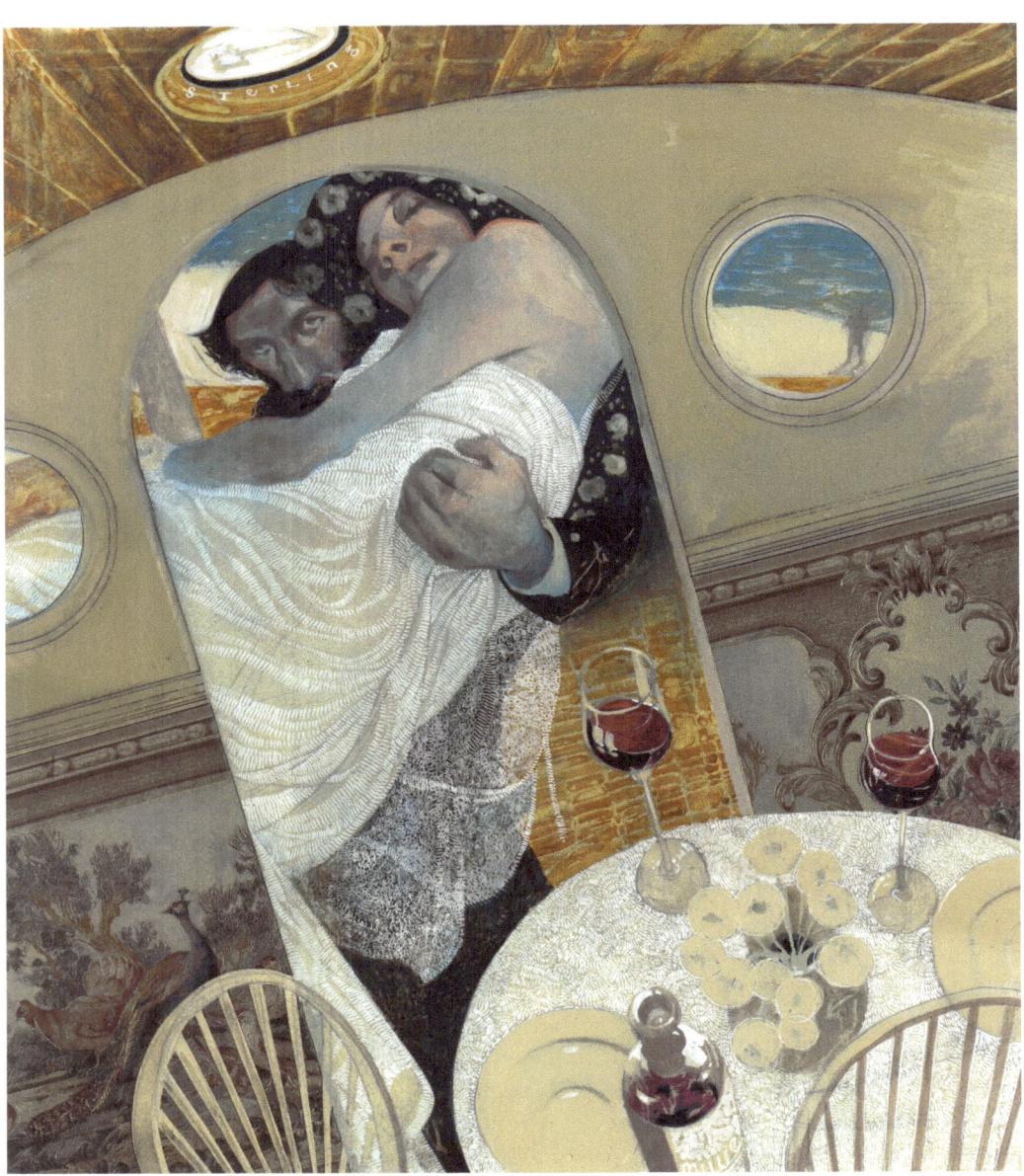

Fig. 14

In a time when the transfer of information has become as natural as breathing and the clashing of cultures sounds more like the sloshing of water, we choose anonymity to avoid accountability, yet strut with the pride and potential of creation. Art is the record of a culture. Will appropriation and the resulting homogenization be the movements that define us?

Popularity, success, and fashion are frequent ringers for quality, but serve better as indicators of accessibility and consensus; the ideal ingredients to yield banality. Folk legends of contemporary art steal from the richness of our history, yet give back nothing. We celebrate their irreverence as if it were charm. Oblivious tolerance of such things is the final marker before reaching the summit of culture and the first to pass on the way back down. Might as well pack up hope and betterment in our sacks as we descend—both born of the pursuit of original thought. No. I politely decline the declination. So I write this as a secessionist of the remix generation. I write this as a record so that these words might be read by someone; anyone. I write this with all the hope that these thoughts are picked up by the same mechanisms that perpetuate the hip, the cool, the trite, and that they may remind someone of the most simple idea—the most important of ideas: original thought exists. Absent the pursuit, original thought simply ceases to be. Its very existence is predicated by the faith in its existence. I fear the consequences of its extinction. Exploration,

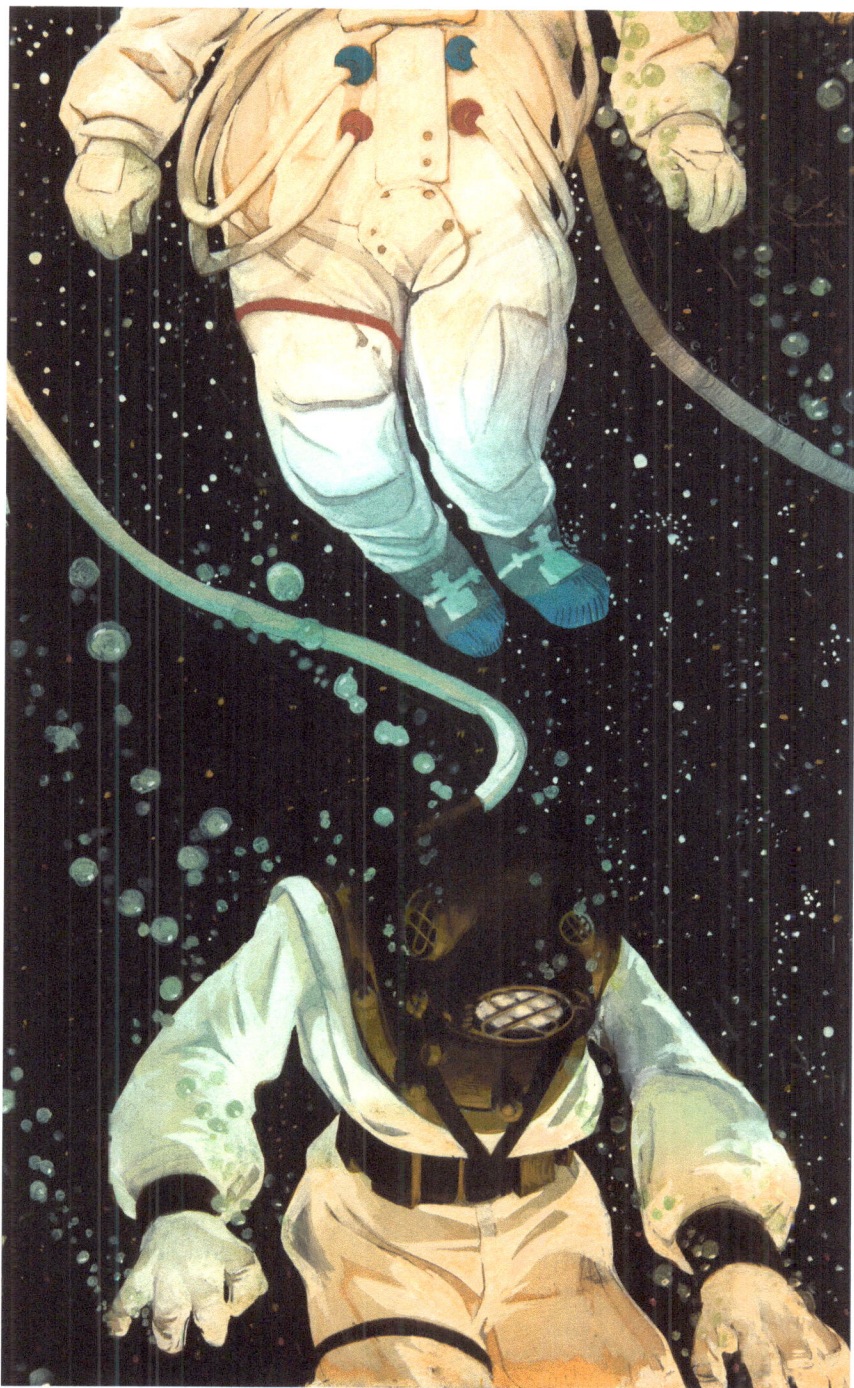

Fig. 15

growth, and evolution of the mind and soul will all fall to the order of unrequited ambition. Throw them in the soup. Line up to be served.

—Sterling Hundley

PEN-AND-INK EDITORIAL ILLUSTRATION: JOHN CUNEO

Despite the many technological and economic changes that have taken place over the past century, the ancient tools of pen and ink provide one of the most effective and potent categories of modern illustration. Today's high-resolution imaging captures subtleties in line and variations in shading that increase the expressiveness of this drawing technique.

Pen-and-ink illustrators now draw with a license that did not exist in Pyle's era. Not only are artists able to personalize their images with nuanced variations in line in ways that would not have been possible 100 years ago, they also depict subjects that were formerly impossible to represent openly. Social criticism from the illustrator's barbed pen has made prejudices and injustices newly visible. Illustrators have also used the intimate nature of line work to represent psychological frankness and sexual candor that were unheard of in Pyle's day (in part because such subject matter would have violated the law.)

John Cuneo's trenchant personal drawings are among the most powerful examples of this phenomenon in illustration today. His sensitive line work has earned him gold and silver medals from his peers at the Society of Illustrators. In 2012, he won the Hamilton King award for the best illustration in the Society's annual show. Largely self-taught, Cuneo began his career handling a wide variety of projects, including greeting cards, and storyboards. He gradually developed his own distinctive voice and today is highly regarded for the humor in his drawings, as well as for his fearless application of artistic freedom in both form and content.

Artist's Statement

It's hardly a straight line from Howard Pyle to here, but I like to think even the Great Man himself would concede that straight lines are overrated. It's all those other lines that concern me and the rest of my pen and ink brethren—all of us who earn our wages putting those lines down on paper with something sharp, black and archival, scratching out a living and all that.

A recent review of a master drawing exhibit in *The New York Times* suggested that in the bountiful feast of the visual arts, painting is the meat, while drawing will always remain just the salad. If this is in fact the case—that painters get all the props and the protein and presumably the pretty girls—why is it that we

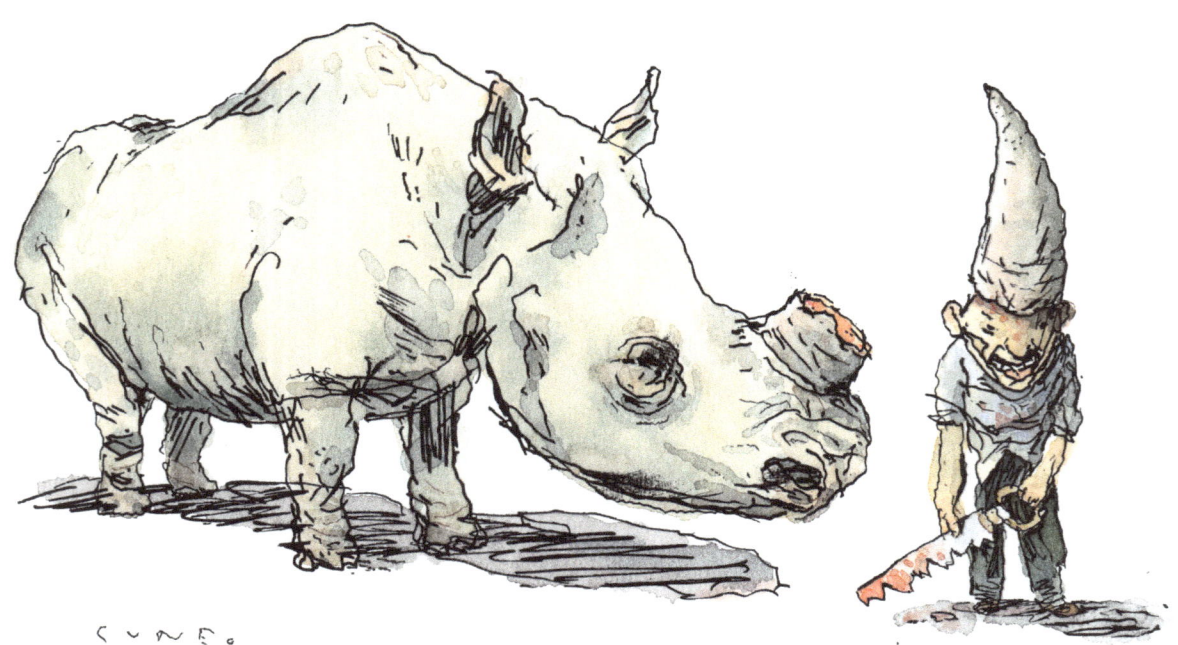

Fig. 16

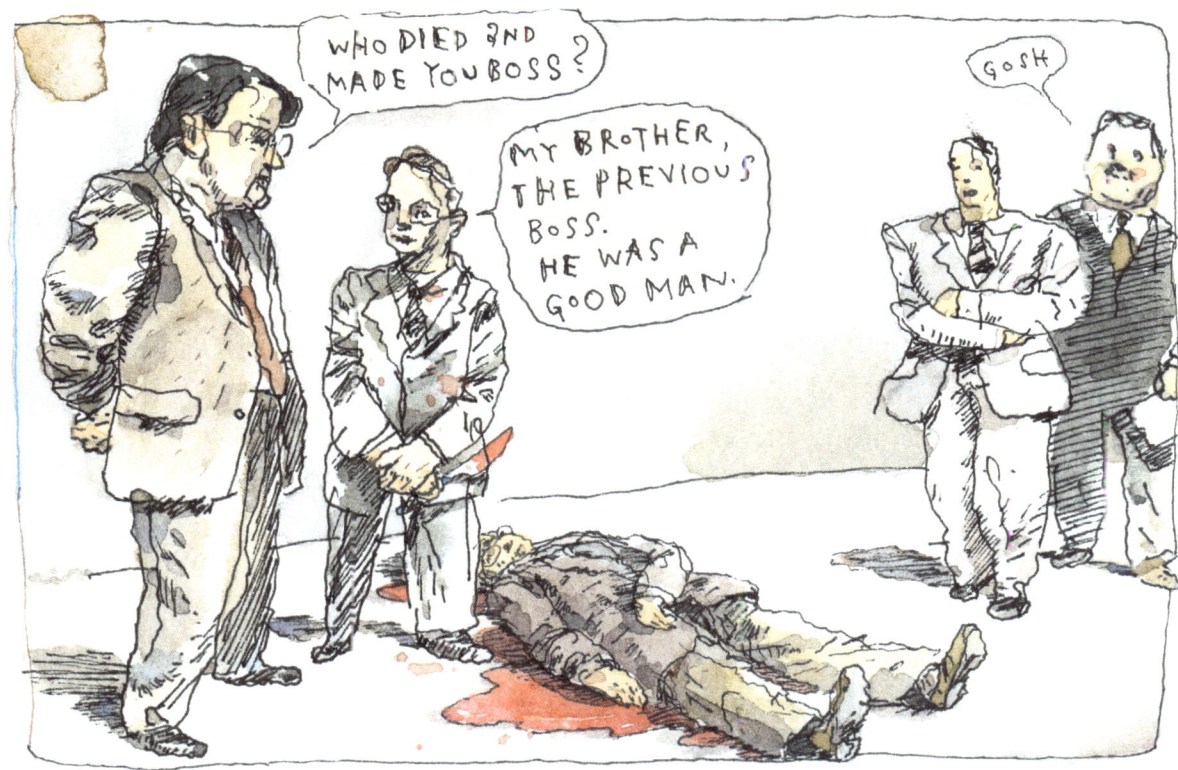

Fig. 17

ink-stained wretches remain hunched over tables dogged y chopping lettuce with a pointy metal stick? Surely there are more respectable, less primitive ways to make a picture—or erasable ways, at the least. So really, why do we draw the line?

Well, I say blame it on the walrus, and/or the carpenter. As much as anything else, an illustrator's approach to picture making is an absorption and reflection of his or her influences. If, like me at a hopelessly impressionable age, you were haunted by the fate, and the crosshatching, of those obliviously doomed oysters and their mournful dining companions, then your own artistic fate was being decided as well. It wasn't all Tenniel's fault; there was plenty of blame to go around. And, in my house, no upper case (A)rt to get in the way. E.H. Shepard's illustrations for *The Wind in the Willows* had me at hello. I don't think I ever read the whole book, but Mr. Toad rappelling out of his Tudor window and down the side the side Toad Hall? Don't even get me started. I was too young to grasp the vaguely racist Southern vernacular in *Uncle Remus*, but I understood those drawings well enough. And A.B. Frost was speaking my language. As were *MAD*, Ronald Searle, and

The New York Times op-ed page in the seventies—Eugene Mihaesco, Roland Topor, Ed Sorel (yes, those were the op-ed salad days).

I grew up convinced that to make black-and-white drawings surrounded by type was the highest of artistic callings. Van Gogh said "every day, a line," but I didn't know him or his work and didn't need the advice anyway. The dye had been cast and it was only one color.

All the great paintings were far away, hanging in museums in a city across a river. By the time I saw my first Sargents or Cornwells up close I was properly astounded but had already taken the vow and was too busy clogging up rapidographs to think about brushes and oils. That's the problem for those of us raised on the salad diet. When somebody finally slaps a porterhouse on our plate, it's too late. We are already full.

—John Cuneo

CHARACTER DESIGN: PETER DE SÈVE

Traditional artistic skills are a significant component of animated films. The powers of observation, imagination, and sense of design that were crucial to 19th century illustration remain so to modern animation. In particular, animated characters are developed from traditional sketches by artists who infuse them with personality.

Peter de Sève works at the crossroads between digital collaboration and pencil drawing. He began as an editorial illustrator in the 1980s. His frequent covers for *The New Yorker* made him famous, but he has also worked for magazines such as *Time, Newsweek, The Atlantic, Smithsonian, Premiere,* and *Entertainment Weekly.* His mastery of facial expressions and imaginative approach led to work as a character designer for animated feature films produced by Disney, Dreamworks, Pixar, and Twentieth Century Fox. De Sève's credits include *Mulan* (1998), *A Bug's Life* (1998), *Monsters* (2001), and the *Ice Age* series of movies (2002–2012). He received the Hamilton King Award from the Society of Illustrators in 2002.

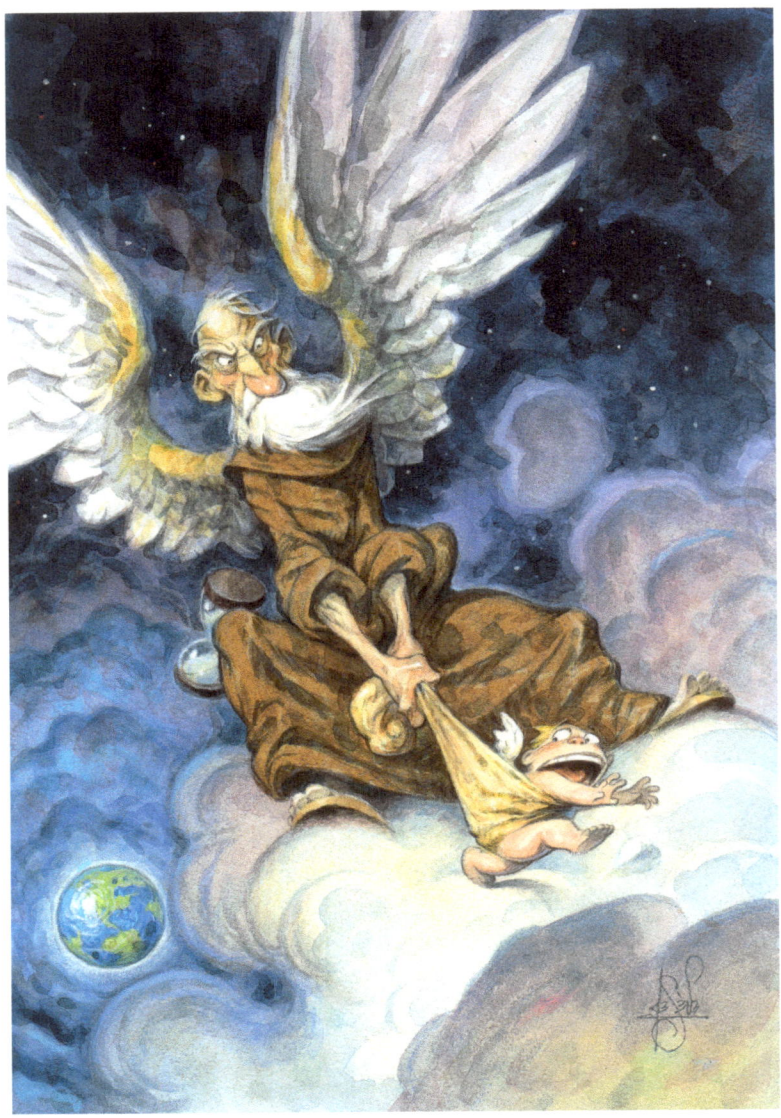

Fig. 18

Artist's Statement

I worked in the trenches for 20 years doing editorial illustrations for countless magazines, including *Forbes, Newsweek, Business Week,* and *The New York Times.* It was pretty demanding and required turning around two or three pieces a week at times. All of which was fabulous training but ultimately exhausting. Somewhere around 1995 I got a call from Walt Disney Feature animation, inviting me to help with the character design for *The Hunchback of Notre Dame,* and, although the drawings went largely ignored, it began my career as a character designer on feature films, which continues to this day.

The invitation came at a perfect time for me, when I was starting to feel a little burned out by the editorial grind. It was a chance to let my sketches do the talking for once and have them be the final work. I always felt that, like most artists I know, my sketches were some of my best work.

I've been asked about the difference between the work I am commissioned to do and the personal art I feel compelled to do. Here is my guilty secret: the work I am commissioned to do is my art. When I am given a job, I bring everything I can to it and when I'm done, I just want to relax.

—Peter de Sève

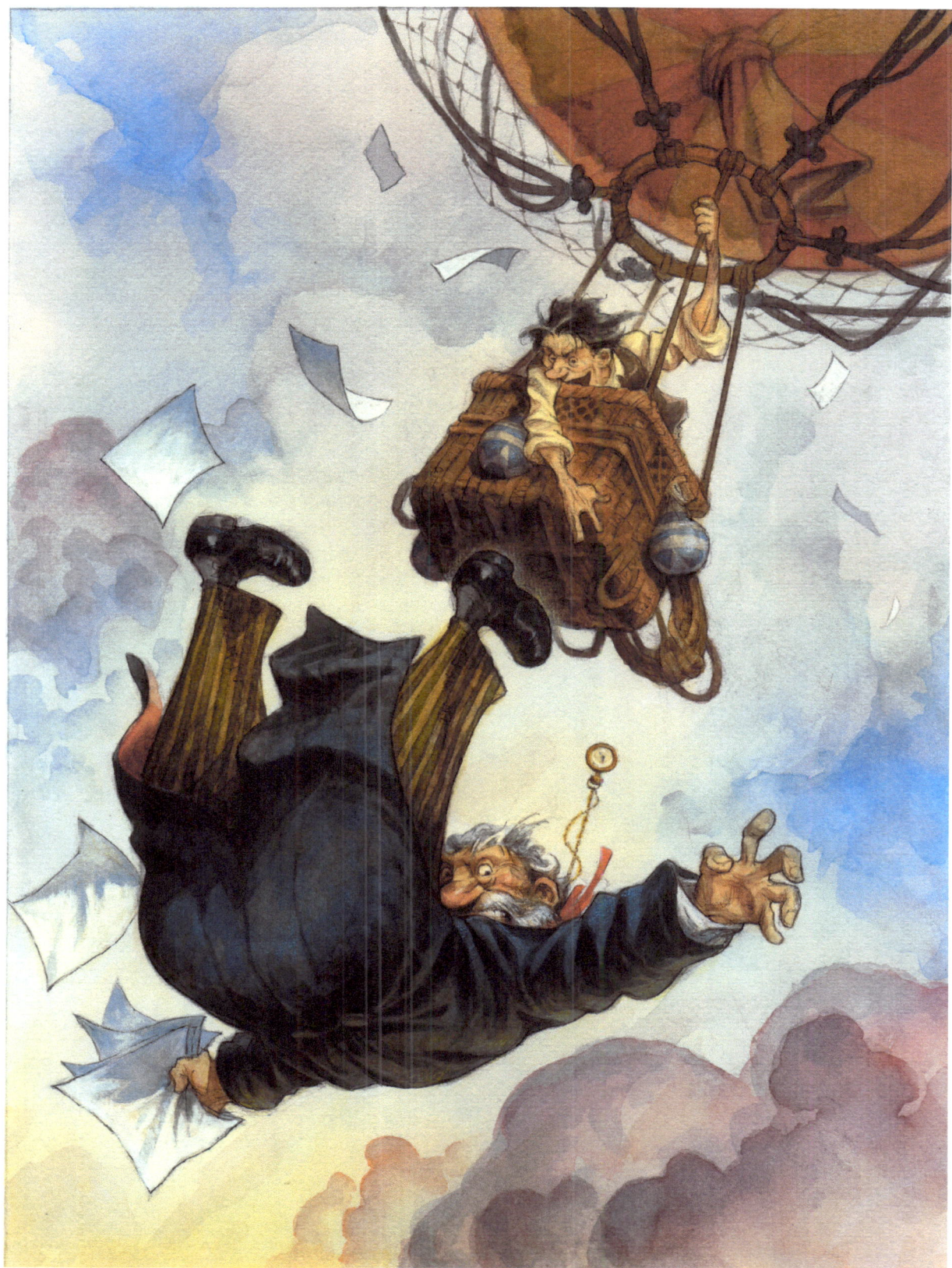

Fig. 19

ANIMATION: RALPH EGGLESTON

Animated feature films are an epic art form in comparison to the individual illustrations of Pyle's era. They can require the collaborative efforts of hundreds of artists, sculptors, writers, computer scientists, electrical engineers, and others who work together to achieve the results the artists envision. Pixar films generally start with a core group of half a dozen creative people who begin at a fairly abstract and intellectual level. The fulfillment of their concepts can grow into a massive enterprise requiring the support of public capital markets (institutional investors and pension funds) to finance production and purchase the hardware and software, along with the distribution networks and other infrastructure. required by animated feature films. Art on this scale, and so heavily dependent on state-of-the-art technology, demands specialized artistic talent to weigh a very different set of trade-offs than those faced by a sole artist working at an easel.

At Pixar, Ralph Eggleston was Art Director for *Toy Story* (1995), the first full-length computer-animated film, as well as for *The Incredibles* (2004) and other films. He was also the Production Designer for Pixar movies, such as *Finding Nemo* (2003) and *Wall•E* (2008).

Artist's Statement

I didn't get into animation because I loved to draw. I got into animation because I loved the stories that could be told, and the responses they could elicit: the final result. Every piece of artwork done leading up to the end result of a story told well is a means to an end—meant to provoke, inspire, and imagine all the possibilities of creating a world for the idea at hand. The collaborative process of making an animated film is the most exciting and challenging part of what I get to do. The contributions of everyone involved leads to work audiences can identify with, share, and enjoy in layers of ways unexpected even to us. When we're successful, they take on a life of their own.

The singular focus on storytelling and character are what I prefer to emphasize. Pretty pictures are nice. But a good idea—clearly communicated to an audience—is my focus. In doing my artwork, the

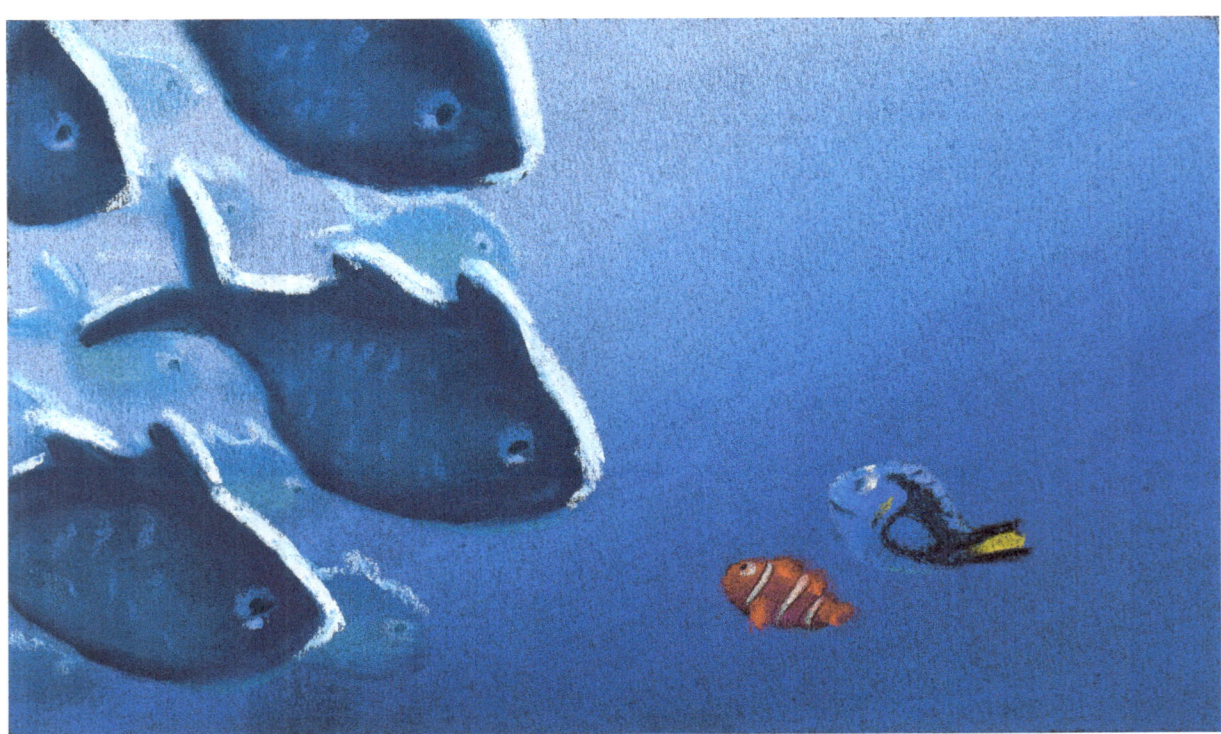

Fig. 20

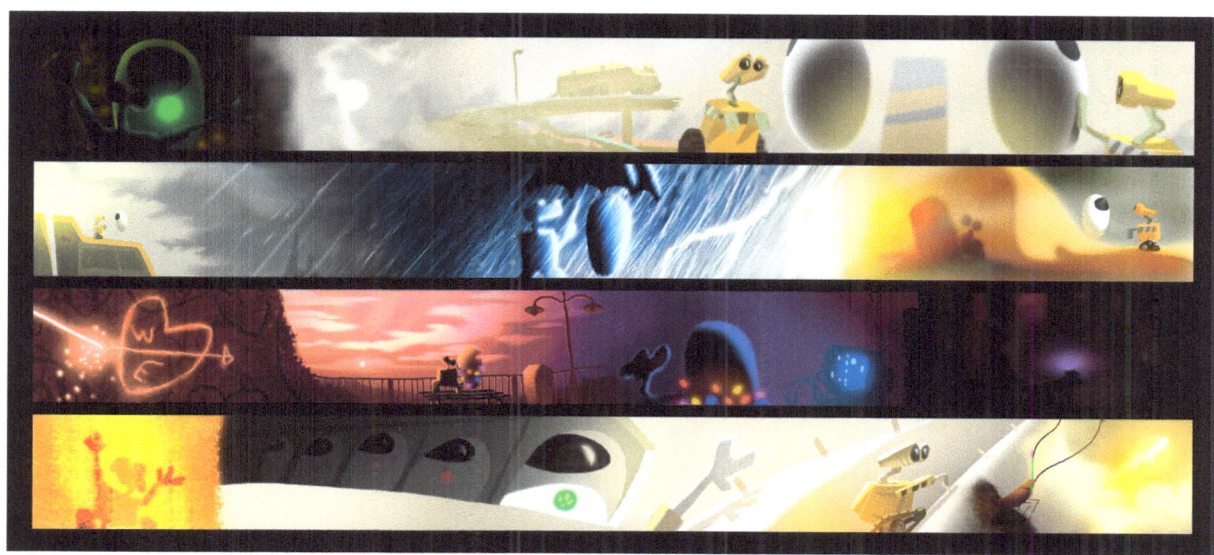

Fig. 21

element of time is foremost in my thoughts. Wasted screen time is an anathema to most film makers, so I approach visuals with the idea of burning into the audience's retina as much information as is needed as clearly and quickly as I can so they can focus on the characters and emotional content of the story they're being told.

While I thoroughly enjoy working in traditional media, like gouache, oil, chalk, and pastel, digital tools such as Photoshop facilitate a quick means to lay out ideas. And, of course, digital tools allow for countless changes as the stories they're supporting develop, change, and improve.

I consider myself lucky to be surrounded by so many talented artists and film makers at Pixar, who continually challenge and inspire me on a daily basis.

—Ralph Eggleston

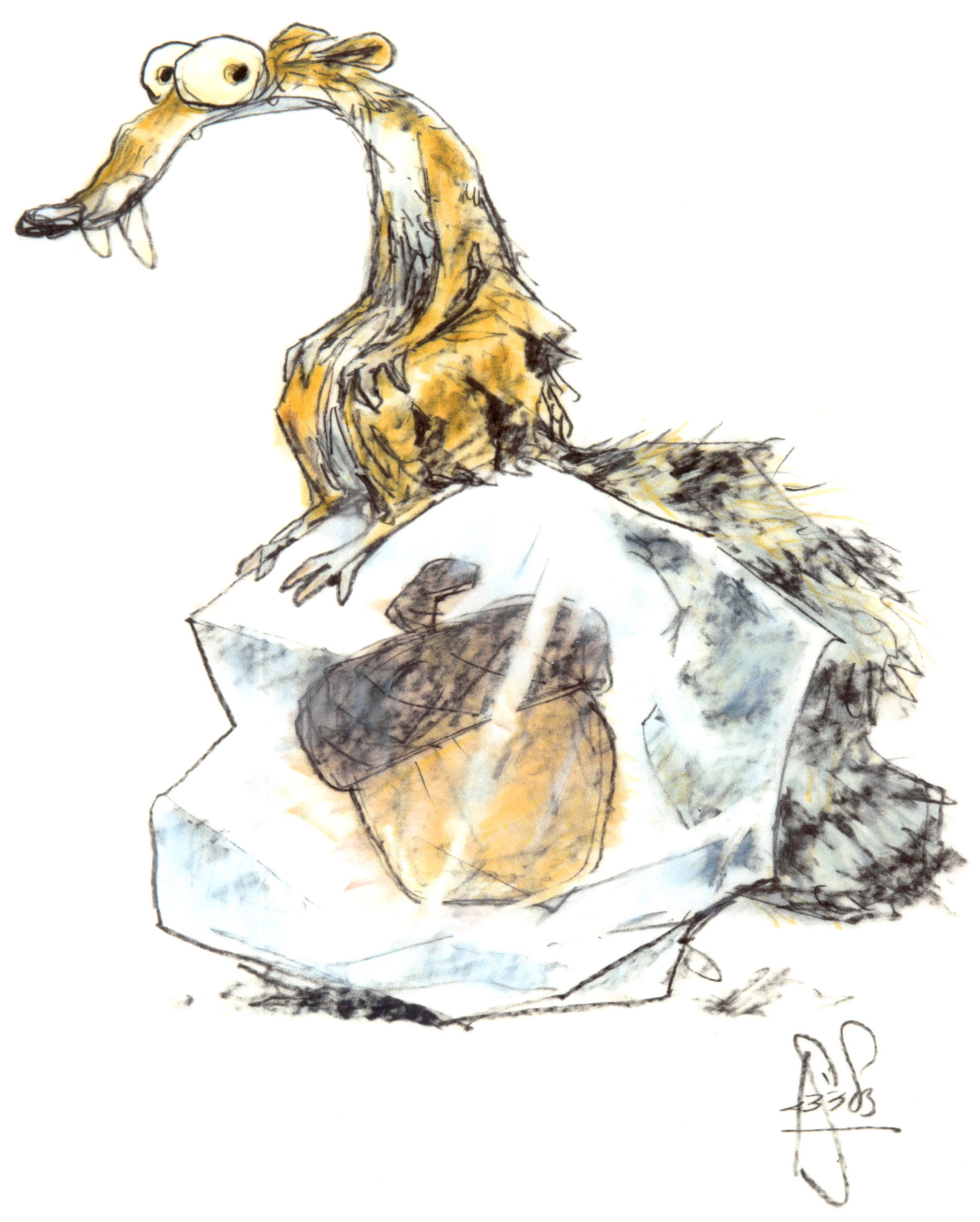

A Century After Howard Pyle

*State of the Art: Illustration 100 Years After
Howard Pyle* presents a representative sampling of
contemporary illustrators who have distinguished
themselves by creating work of enduring artistic
value. While their art is grounded in the historical
world of design and composition, of sensitive line
and expressive color, they also participate in the
arena of mass media and modern communications
technologies.

The field of illustration will continue to evolve
as its technologies, commercial objectives, and
demographics change. Many illustrators today devote
less attention to learning anatomy, perspective,
and the other conventional skills of Howard Pyle's
day. Images are often begun by "photoshopping"
a photograph rather than sketching with charcoal.
Artists do not need to develop techniques with
traditional media, as software has become more
sophisticated at simulating pencil line, oil paint,
or watercolor. Already, cutting-edge talents in
the gaming and movie industries are developing
reputations for themselves with computer-based
tools that will require us to rethink our standards of
artistic excellence. But at this point in the rich history
of illustration, it is safe to recognize and celebrate the
achievements of master illustrators such as the eight
featured in this exhibition.

1 Christine Podmaniczky, personal communication to the author, May 12, 2012.
2 Robert Weaver, quoted in *Innovators of American Illustration*, edited by Steven Heller (New York: Van Nostrand Reinhold Company, 1986), page 7
3 Ivan Rzal, "Interview with Rob Janoff, Designer of the Apple Logo." *Creativebits*. August 3, 2009. Web. November 30, 2012.
   http://www.creativebits.org/interivew/interview_rob_janoff_designer_apple_logo.
4 Austin Briggs, in Walt and Roger Reed, *The Illustrator in America, 1880–1980* (New York: Madison Square Press, 1984), page 252.
5 Walt Reed, in Walt and Roger Reed, *The Illustrator in America, 1880–1980* (New York: Madison Square Press, 1984), page 291.
6 Milton Glaser, *Art Is Work* (New York: The Overlook Press, 2000), page 11.

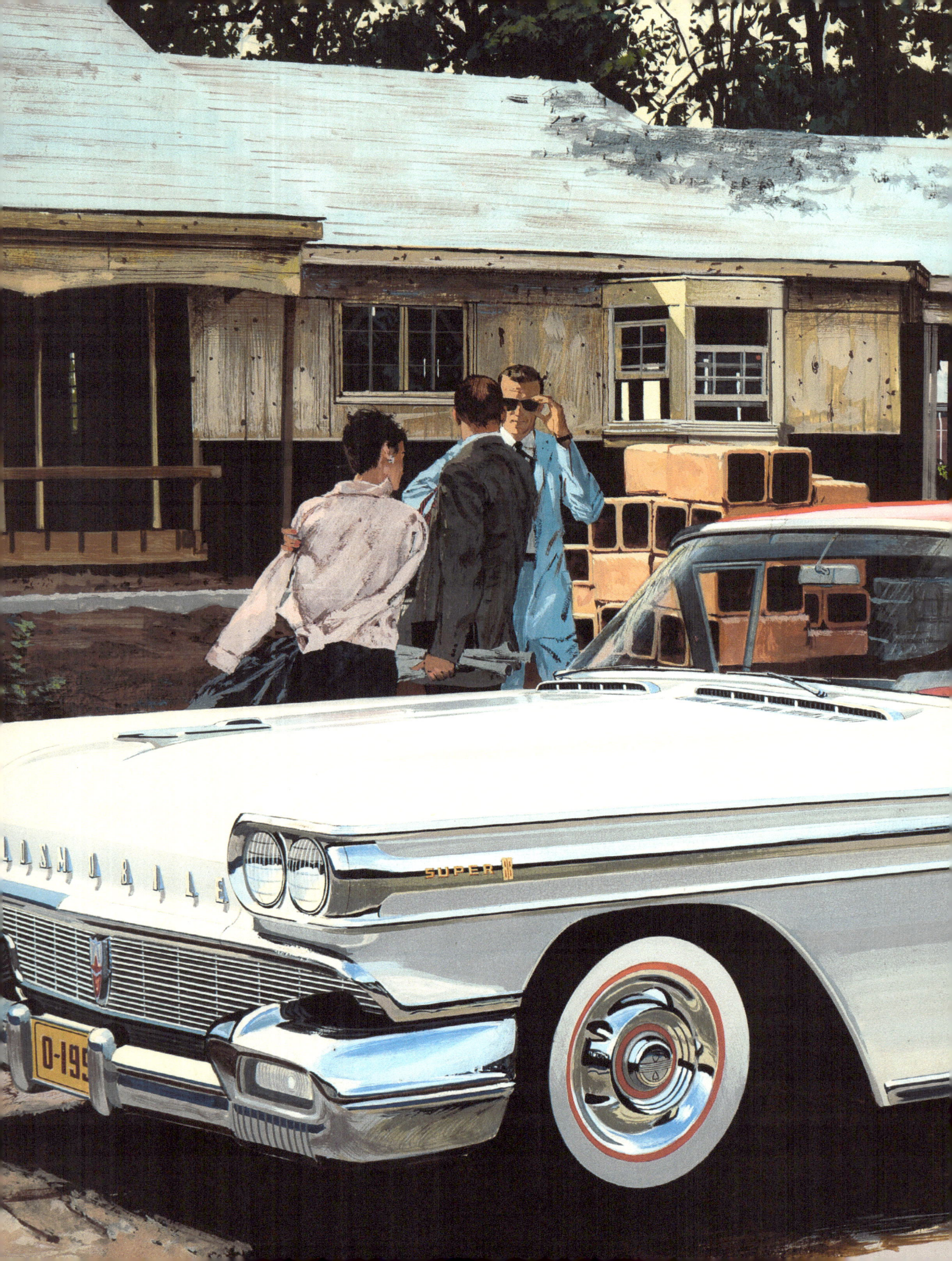

FIGURE 1

Theophylact Bache Saving Graydon from the Mob in 1776, 1882, for "Old New York Coffee Houses," by John Austin Stephens, in *Harper s New Monthly Magazine,* March 1882. Howard Py e (1853–1911). Ink, ink wash, and gouache on paper, 8 5/8 x 12 inches. Delaware Art Museum, Gayle and Alene Hoskins Endowment Fund, 2012.

FIGURE 2

Woodblock for *Theophylact Bache Saving Graydon from the Mob in 1776,* by Howard Pyle, for "Old New York Coffee Houses," by John Austin Stephers, in *Harper's New Monthly Magazine,* March 1882. J. P. Davis (active 1867–1882). Woodblock, 3 3/4 x 12 inches. Delaware Art Museum, Gayle and Alene Hoskins Endowment Fund, 2012.

FIGURE 3

Detail of figure 2. The signature of the engraver J. P. Dav s is visible in the woodblock.

FIGURE 4

The Buccaneer was a Picturesque Fellow for "The Fate of a Treasure Town," *1905,* by Howard Pyle, in *Harper's Monthly Magazine,* December 1905. Howard Pyle (1853–1911). Oil on canvas. 30 1/2 x 19 1/2 inches. Delaware Art Museum, Museum Purchase, 1912.

FIGURE 5

Recruitment poster for the United States Army, 1917. James Montgomery Flagg (1877–1950). Lithograph on paper, 40 x 30 inches. Delaware Art Museum.

FIGURE 6

Their happiness was all mixed up with being young, 1959, for "A Small Miracle," by Mary Augusta Rodgers, n *McCall's,* June 1959. Bernie Fuchs (1932–2009). Gouache on illustration board, 17 1/4 x 19 1/2 inches. Collection of Anna Lee Fuchs.

FIGURE 7

Suicide, 1984, for "A Twilight's Last Gleam ng," by Frank Deford in *Sports Illustrated,* November 19, 1984. Bernie Fuchs (1932–2009). Oil on canvas, 22 3/4 x 32 inches. Private Collection.

FIGURE 8

Angel Alley, 1978, album cover for Linda Cohen. Tomato Records, 1978. Milton Glaser (B. 1929) Pen and ink on paper, 13 7/8 x 18 5/8 inches. Collection of the artist.

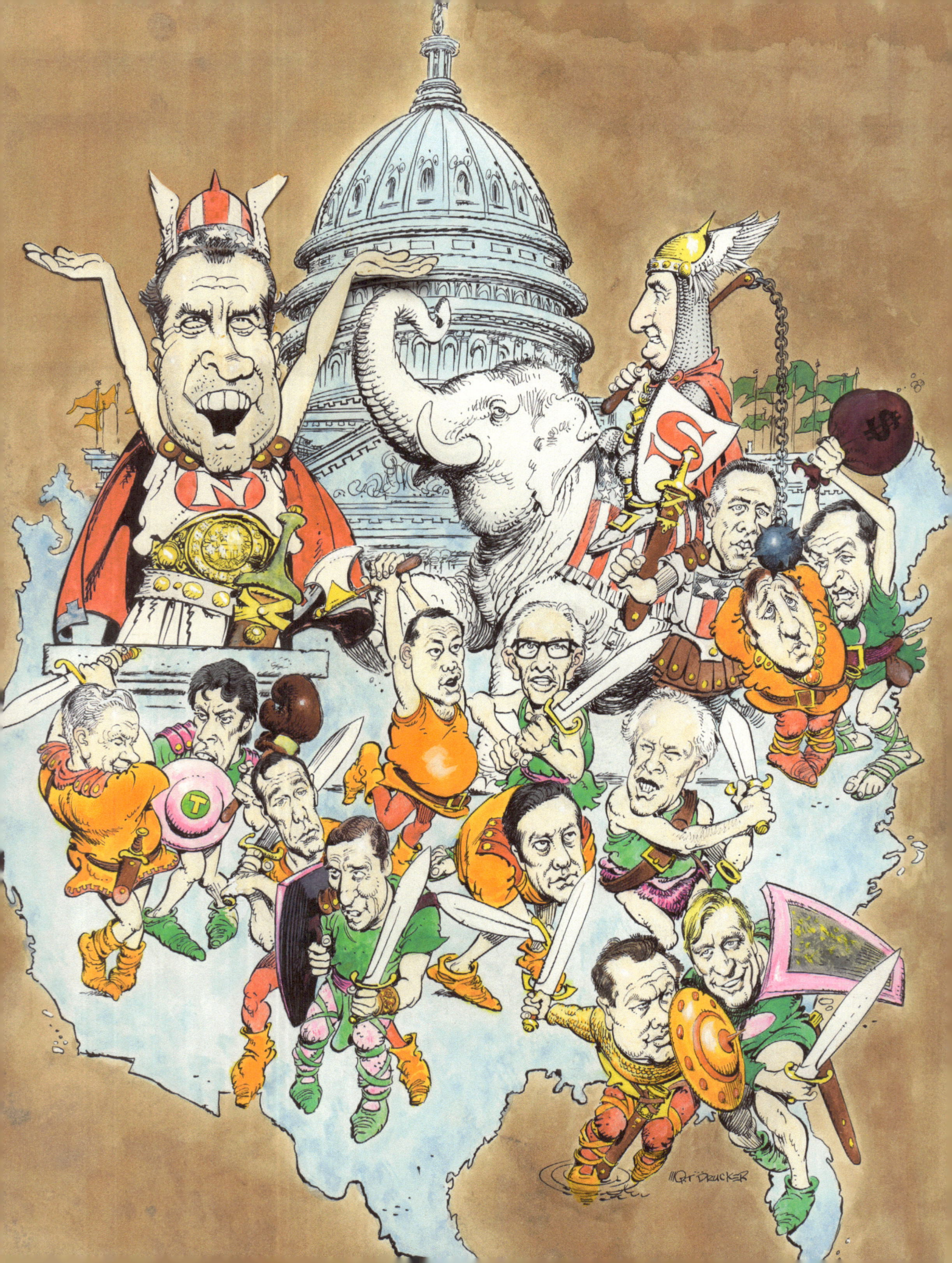

FIGURE 9

Only Words, poster for School of Visual Arts, 1985. Milton Glaser (B. 1929). Offset lithograph on paper, 45 x 29 1/2 inches. Milton Glaser Design Study Center and Archives, School of Visual Arts.

FIGURE 10

The Odd Father, for *MAD,* December 1972. Mort Drucker (B. 1929). Ink on illustration board, 11 1/2 x 28 inches. Private Collection, © Mort Drucker.

FIGURE 11

Put*on, for *MAD,* January 1971. Mort Drucker (B. 1929). Ink on illustration board, 25 1/2 x 20 inches. Private Collection, © Mort Drucker.

FIGURE 12

Flesheaters require, 2008. Phil Hale (B. 1963). Oil on linen, 38 x 50 x 1 1/2 inches. Collection of the artist, © Phil Hale 2012.

FIGURE 13

Secession, 2001, cover for *Goad, The Many Moods of Phil Hale* (New Hampshire: Donald M. Grant, 2001). Phil Hale (B. 1963). Oil on linen, 50 x 62 inches. Collection of Robert K. Wiener, © Phil Hale 2012.

FIGURE 14

Shipwreck, 2007, for *Viginia Living Magazine,* June 2007. Sterling Hundley (B. 1976). Acrylic, ink, gouache, and collage on board, 16 1/4 x 14 inches. Collection of the artist.

FIGURE 15

Vertical Hold, 2009, for the Illustration Academy. Sterling Hundley (B. 1976). Acrylic, gouache, ink, pencil, and watercolor on illustration board, 20 x 12 15/16 inches. Private Collection.

FIGURE 16

Poacher, 2010. John Cuneo (b. 1957). Pen, ink, copy toner, and watercolor on paper, 8 x 10 1/2 inches. Collection of the artist, © 2004 – 2012, John Cuneo. All Rights Reserved.

FIGURE 17

Who Died and Made You Boss?, 2011. John Cuneo (b. 1957). Pen, ink, and watercolor on paper, 3 1/2 x 5 1/4 inches. Collection of the artist, © 2004–2012, John Cuneo. All Rights Reserved.

FIGURE 18

Auld L' Anxiety, unpublished cover for *The New Yorker,* October 2005. Peter de Sève (B. 1958). Watercolor, colored pencil, and ink on paper, 15 1/2 x 10 1/2 inches. Collection of the artist.

FIGURE 19

"So I hove him out of the balloon!", from *A Murder, a Mystery, and a Marriage,* by Mark Twain (New York: W. W. Norton & Company, 2001). Peter de Sève (B. 1958). Watercolor, colored pencil, and ink on paper, 13 x 9 3/4 inches. Collection of the artist.

FIGURE 20

School, sequence pastel for *Finding Nemo* (Pixar Animation Studios, 2003). Ralph Eggleston (B. 1965). Pastel on paper, 6 x 8 inches. Artwork provided by Pixar Animation Studio.

FIGURE 21

Colorscript for WALL • E (Pixar Animation Studios and Walt Disney Pictures, 2008). Ralph Eggleston (B. 1965). Digital painting, 13 1/2 x 30 inches. Artwork provided by Pixar Animation Studio.

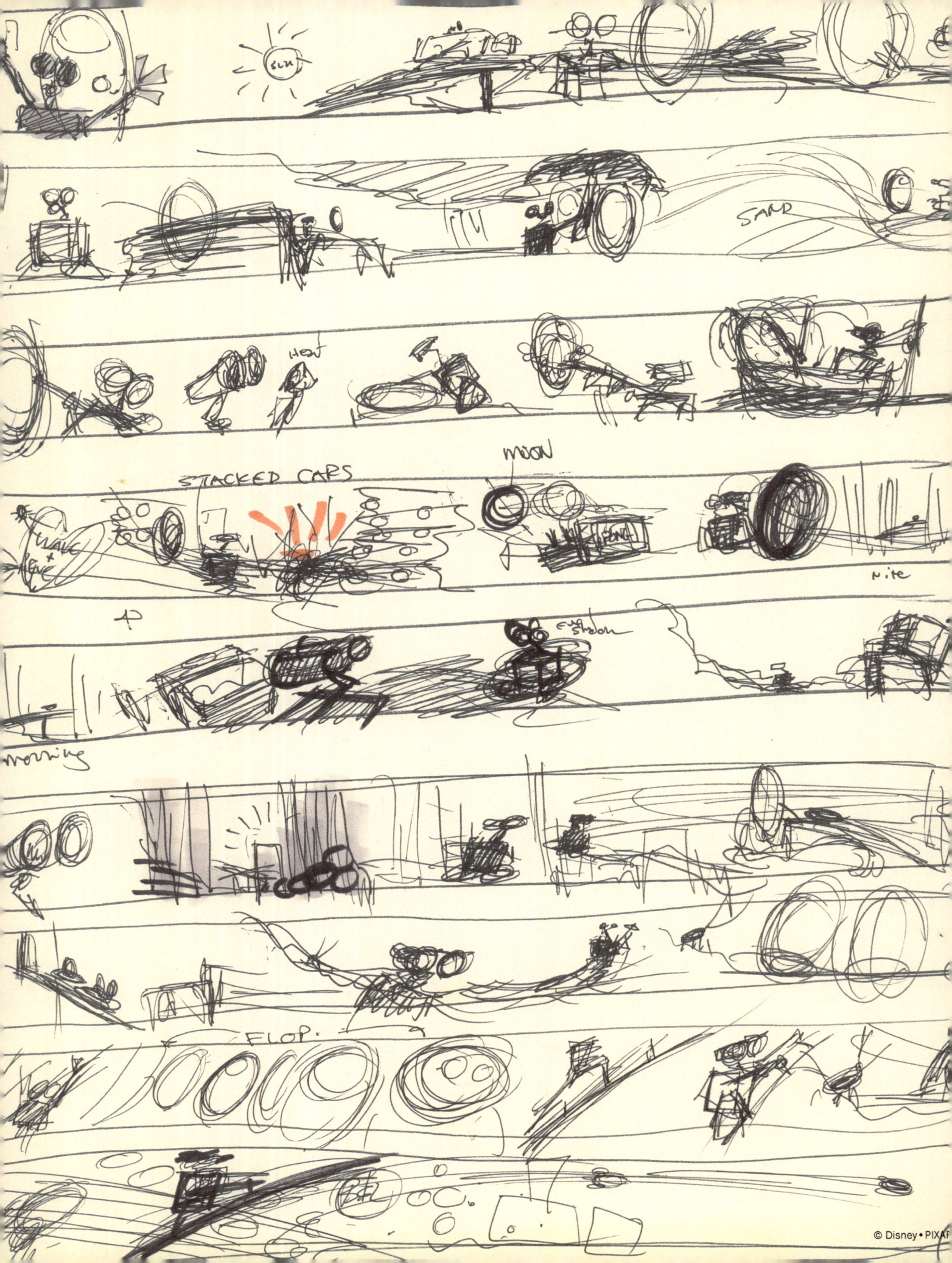

EXHIBITION CHECKLIST

BERNIE FUCHS (1932 – 2009)

1   *Oldsmobile Super 88,* 1958, advertisement
for Oldsmobile
Gouache on illustration board, 18 x 26 3/4 inches
Collection of Anna Lee Fuchs

2   *Their happiness was all mixed up with being
young,* 1959, for "A Small Miracle," by Mary
Augusta Rodgers, in *McCall's,* June 1959
Gouache on illustration board, 17 1/4 x
19 1/2 inches
Collection of Anna Lee Fuchs

3   *Both the aging woman and the old car were
beautiful to the young man,* 1963, for "The Rivals,"
by Lucinda Baker, in *Redbook,* November 1963
Gouache on illustration board, 16 x 22 7/8 inches
Collection of Anna Lee Fuchs

4   *The March,* 1967, for "The March," by
Carson McCullers, in *Redbook,* March 1967
Mixed media on board, 26 x 32 inches
Collection of the Society of Illustrators,
donated by the artist (069.017)

5   *Pablo Casals at Home,* 1970, for "La Nueva
Vida," in *Lithopinion Magazine,* Summer 1970
Oil on illustration board, 20 x 30 inches
Collection of Anna Lee Fuchs

6   *Matador,* c. 1980
Lithograph on paper, 25 x 20 inches
Collection of Anna Lee Fuchs

7   *Fearsome Foursome,* early 1980's
Oil on canvas, 31 x 50 inches
Collection of Anna Lee Fuchs

8   *Suicide,* 1984, for "A Twilight's Last Gleaming,"
by Frank Deford, in *Sports Illustrated,*
November 19, 1984
Oil on canvas, 22 3/4 x 32 inches
Private Collection

MILTON GLASER (B. 1929)

9   *Hermann Hesse and Family,* 1974, for *Hermann
Hesse 1975 Calendar* (New York: Farrar, Straus
and Giroux, Inc., 1975)
Line drawing with colored adhesive on illustration
board, 12 3/4 x 13 inches
Collection of the artist

10   *Angel Alley,* 1978, album cover for Linda Cohen,
Tomato Records, 1978
Pen and ink on paper, 13 7/8 x 18 5/8 inches
Collection of the artist

11   *Feel the Heat,* 1979, album cover for Kathi
Baker, Tomato Records, 1979
Ink and wash on paper, 12 1/8 x 16 inches
Collection of the artist

12   *Only Words,* sketch for poster for School of
Visual Arts, 1985
Pen and colored ink on paper, 18 x 14 1/2 inches
Milton Glaser Design Study Center and Archives,
School of Visual Arts

13   *Only Words,* poster for School of Visual Arts,
1985
Offset lithograph on paper, 45 x 29 1/2 inches
Milton Glaser Design Study Center and Archives,
School of Visual Arts

14   *Dante Ascending,* 1999, for *La Divina
Commedia: Purgatorio* (Milan: Nuages, 1999)
Monoprint on paper, 22 x 14 7/8 inches
Collection of the artist

15   *Dante and Flames,* 1999, *for La Divina
Commedia: Purgatorio* (Milan: Nuages, 1999)
Monoprint on paper, 22 x 14 7/8 inches
Collection of the artist

16   *Angels and Devils,* 1999, for *La Divina
Commedia: Purgatorio* (Milan: Nuages, 1999)
Monoprint on paper, 22 x 14 7/8 inches
Collection of the artist

17   *Untitled,* second study for cover of *The Atlantic,*
not dated
Colored inks on cardboard, 12 1/2 x 10 inches
Milton Glaser Design Study Center and Archives,
School of Visual Arts

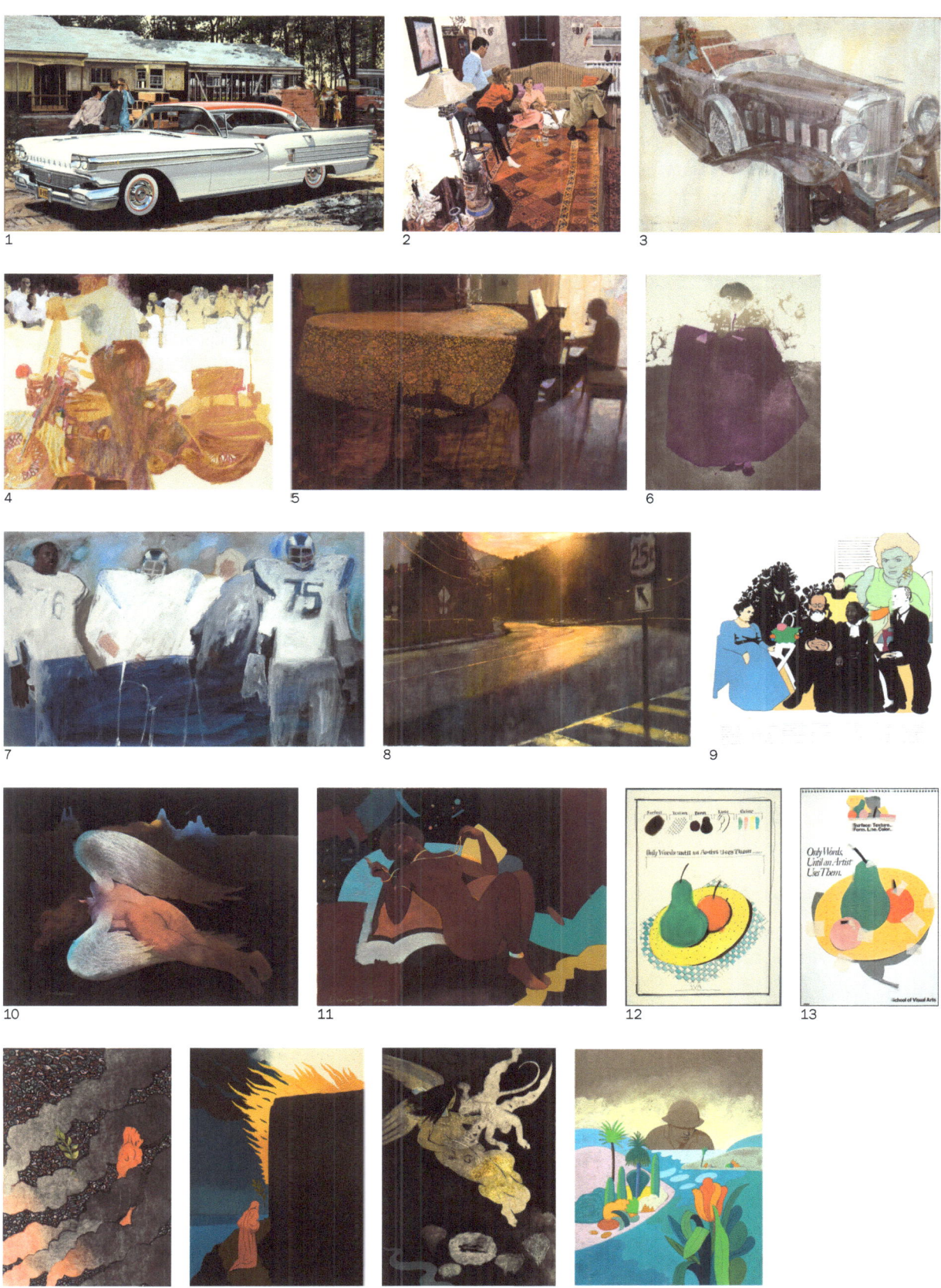

MORT DRUCKER (B. 1929)

18 *Battle for the Senate,* 1970, cover for *TIME,*
    October 26, 1970
    Watercolor and ink on board, 24 3/4 x 18 1/8 inches
    National Portrait Gallery, Smithsonian Institution;
    gift of *TIME* magazine, © Mort Drucker.
    National Portrait Gallery, Smithsonian Institution /
    Art Resources, NY

19 *Put*on,* for *MAD,* January 1971
    Ink on illustration board, 25 1/2 x 20 inches
    Private Collection, © Mort Drucker

20 *The Odd Father,* for *MAD,* December 1972
    Ink and ink wash on illustration board,
    24 3/8 x 18 inches
    Private Collection, © Mort Drucker

21 *Bobby Riggs,* 1973, cover for *TIME,*
    September 10, 1973
    Watercolor and ink on paper, 18 1/2 x
    12 1/4 inches
    National Portrait Gallery, Smithsonian Institution;
    gift of *TIME* magazine, © Mort Drucker.
    National Portrait Gallery, Smithsonian Institution /
    Art Resources, NY

22 *The Odd Father,* for *MAD,* December 1972
    Ink on illustration board, 11 1/2 x 28 inches
    Private Collection, © Mort Drucker

23 *The Shootiest,* for *MAD,* April 1977
    Ink on illustration board, 20 1/8 x 18 3/4 inches
    Private Collection, © Mort Drucker

24 *Fearless Bueller's Day Off,* for *MAD,* January 1987
    Ink on illustration board, 23 15/16 x
    35 5/8 inches
    Private Collection, © Mort Drucker

25 *Beverly Hills Slop, Too!,* for *MAD,* December 1987
    Ink on illustration board, 18 1/4 x 32 1/2 inches
    Private Collection, © Mort Drucker

PHIL HALE (B. 1963)

26 *Haetmiser,* 1998
    Oil on linen, 20 x 20 inches
    Collection of John and Lori Butler, © Phil Hale
    2012

27 *Secession,* 2001, cover for *Goad, The Many
    Moods of Phil Hale* (New Hampshire:
    Donald M. Grant, 2001)
    Oil on linen, 50 x 62 inches
    Collection of Robert K. Wiener, © Phil Hale 2012

28 *Mockingbirds,* 2005
    Oil on linen, 50 x 50 inches
    Collection of the artist, © Phil Hale 2012

29 *Incur,* 2006
    Oil on linen, 48 x 48 inches
    Private Collection, © Phil Hale 2012

30 *Destr,* 2006/2011
    Oil on linen, 52 x 48 inches
    Collection of Robert K. Wiener, © Phil Hale 2012

31 *Lord Jim,* 2007, cover for *Lord Jim,* by Joseph
    Conrad (London: Penguin Classics, 2007)
    Oil on linen, 33 x 33 inches
    Private Collection, © Phil Hale 2012

32 *Nostromo,* 2007, cover for *Nostromo,* by Joseph
    Conrad (London: Penguin Classics, 2007)
    Oil on linen, 33 x 33 inches
    Private Collection, © Phil Hale 2012

33 *Flesheaters require,* 2008
    Oil on linen, 38 x 50 inches
    Collection of the artist, © Phil Hale 2012

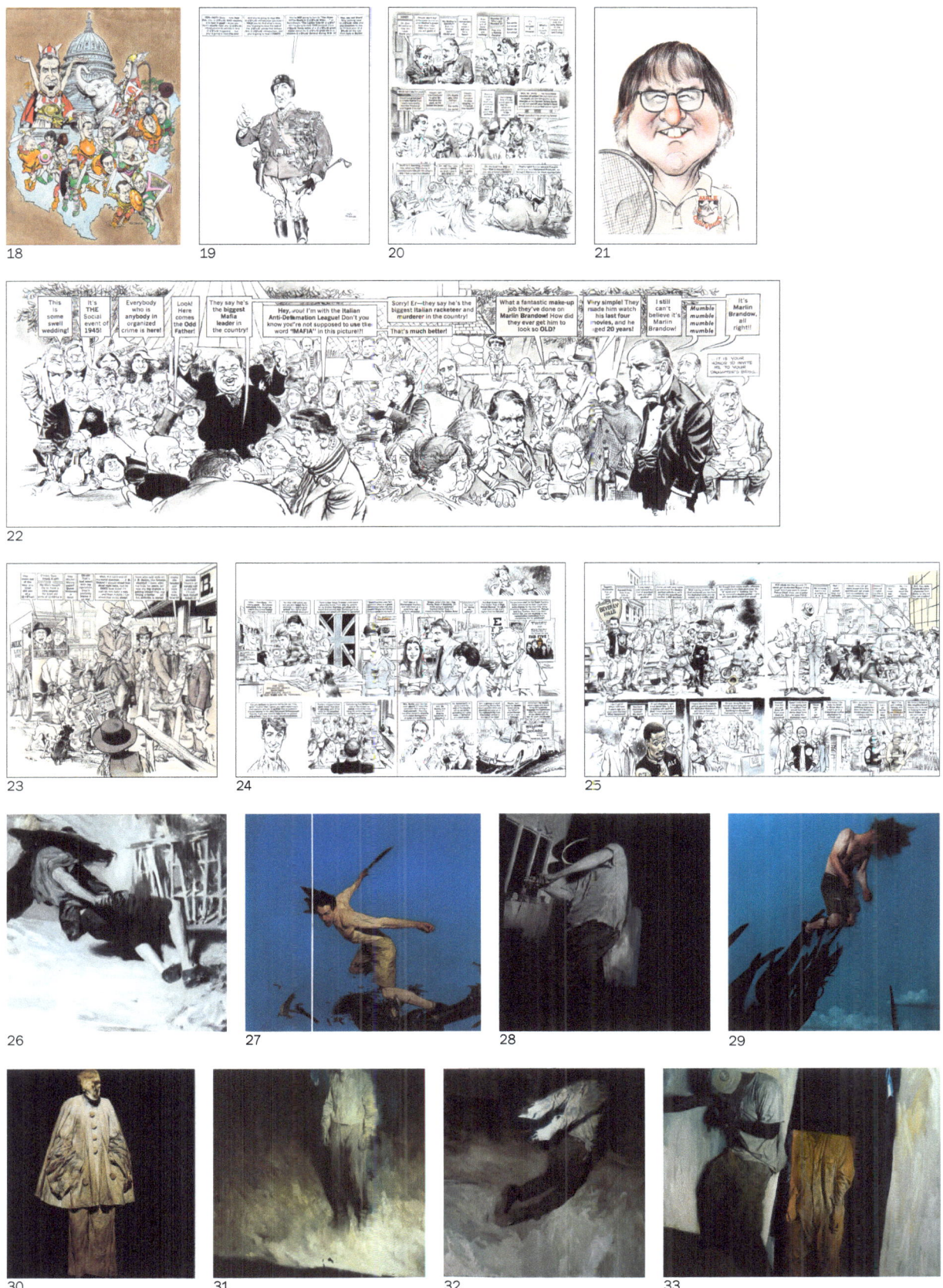

STERLING HUNDLEY (B. 1976)

34   *Hair,* 2006, poster for Rockwell Theater,
     Pittsburgh Playhouse, Point Park University
     Acrylic, ink, and gouache on board,
     20 x 13 3/4 inches
     Collection of the artist

35   *The Skin of Our Teeth,* 2006, poster for
     Pittsburgh Playhouse, Point Park University
     Acrylic, ink, and gouache on illustration board,
     13 x 18 3/4 inches
     Collection of the artist

36   *Shipwreck,* 2007, for *Virginia Living Magazine,*
     June 2007
     Gouache, ink, pencil, watercolor, and collage on
     board, 16 1/4 x 14 inches
     Collection of the artist

37   *William Henry Harrison,* 2007, for "William
     Henry Harrison," in *Virginia Living Magazine,*
     February 2007
     Acrylic, gouache, and watercolor on illustration
     board, 20 7/8 x 16 inches
     Private Collection

38   *Gibson's Gal,* 2008, for "Gibson's Gal to
     Gibson's Girl," in *Virginia Living Magazine,* April 2008
     Gouache, ink, pencil, and watercolor on
     illustration board, 20 x 14 ½ inches
     Private Collection

39   *Vertical Hold,* 2009, for the Illustration Academy
     Acrylic, gouache, and watercolor on illustration
     board, 20 x 12 15/16 inches
     Private Collection

40   *The Pearl Fishers,* 2011, poster for the Lyric
     Opera of Kansas City
     Acrylic, gouache, and watercolor on illustration
     board, 12 x 8 1/4 inches
     Private Collection

41   *A Fruitless Endeavor,* 2012
     Ink and tape on cardboard panel, 20 x 16 inches
     Collection of the artist

JOHN CUNEO (B. 1957)

42   *Untitled,* unpublished illustration for *Runner's
     World,* 2009
     Pen, ink, copy toner, and watercolor on paper,
     4 1/2 x 6 inches
     Collection of the artist, © 2004–2012,
     John Cuneo. All Rights Reserved

43   *Guys and Dolls,* 2010
     Pen, ink, and watercolor on paper,
     9 3/4 x 10 inches
     Private Collection, © 2004–2012, John Cuneo.
     All Rights Reserved

44   *Poacher,* 2010
     Pen, ink, copy toner, and watercolor on paper,
     8 x 10 1/2 inches
     Collection of the artist, © 2004–2012,
     John Cuneo. All Rights Reserved

45   *Why I quit drinking,* 2010
     Pen, ink, copy toner, and watercolor on paper,
     13 1/2 x 8 1/2 inches
     Collection of the artist, © 2004–2012,
     John Cuneo. All Rights Reserved

46   *Gator Bait,* 2011
     Pen, ink, copy toner, and watercolor on paper,
     6 1/2 x 8 1/4 inches
     Collection of the artist, © 2004–2012,
     John Cuneo. All Rights Reserved

47   *Untitled,* 2011
     Pen, ink, and watercolor on paper, 8 x 9 inches
     Collection of the artist, © 2004–2012,
     John Cuneo. All Rights Reserved

48   *Who Died and Made You Boss?,* 2011
     Pen, ink, and watercolor on paper,
     3 1/2 x 5 1/4 inches
     Collection of the artist, © 2004–2012,
     John Cuneo. All Rights Reserved

49   *Philip Larkin and Bob Dylan go antiquing,* 2011
     Pen, ink, and watercolor on paper, 8 1/2 x 7 inches
     Collection of the artist, © 2004–2012,
     John Cuneo. All Rights Reserved

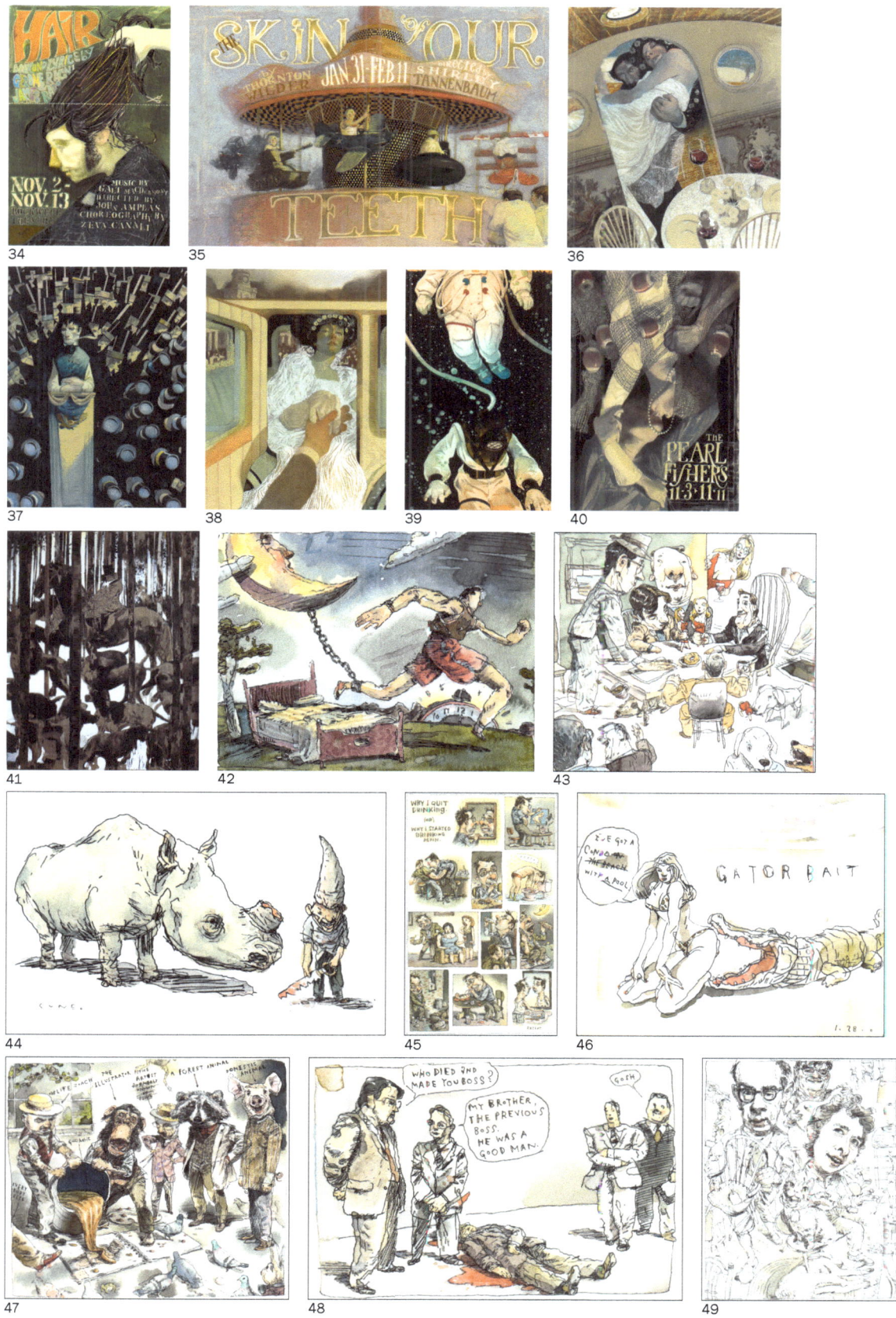

PETER DE SÈVE (B. 1958)

50 *Tailed,* cover for *The New Yorker,* January 24, 1994
Watercolor, colored pencil, and ink on paper,
14 3/4 x 11 inches
Collection of the artist

51 *Auld L' Anxiety,* unpublished cover for *The New Yorker,* October 2005
Watercolor, colored pencil, and ink on paper,
15 1/2 x 10 1/2 inches
Collection of the artist

52 *Local Heroes,* cover for *The New Yorker,*
October 29, 2001
Watercolor, colored pencil, and ink on paper,
14 1/2 x 10 1/4 inches
Collection of the artist

53 *"So I hove him out of the balloon!",* 2001, from
A Murder, a Mystery, and a Marriage, by Mark
Twain (New York: W.W. Norton & Company, 2001)
Watercolor, colored pencil, and ink on paper,
13 x 9 3/4 inches
Collection of the artist

54 *Call for Entries,* 2002, poster for the Society of
Illustrators, New York
Watercolor, colored pencil, and ink on paper,
13 x 13 inches
Collection of the artist

55 *Uncle Fungus,* character study for *Ice Age:
Continental Drift* (Twentieth Century Fox Film
Corporation, 2009)
Wax pastel crayon on parchment tracing paper,
17 x 14 inches
TM & © 2012, Twentieth Century Fox Film
Corporation. All rights reserved.

56 *Scrat,* character study for *Ice Age* figure
(Twentieth Century Fox Film Corporation, 2009)
Wax pastel crayon on polyester film,
15 x 11 1/2 inches
TM & © 2012, Twentieth Century Fox Film
Corporation. All rights reserved.

57 *Sirens,* character study for *Ice Age: Continental
Drift* (Twentieth Century Fox Film Corporation,
2009)
Wax pastel crayon on polyester film,
17 x 14 inches
TM & © 2012, Twentieth Century Fox Film
Corporation. All rights reserved.

RALPH EGGLESTON (B. 1965)

58 *School,* sequence pastel for *Finding Nemo* (Pixar
Animation Studios, 2003)
Pastel on paper, 6 x 8 inches
Artwork provided by Pixar Animation Studio

59 *Pelicans,* sequence pastel for *Finding Nemo*
(Pixar Animation Studios, 2003)
Pastel on paper, 4 1/2 x 6 inches, 5 x 6 inches
Artwork provided by Pixar Animation Studio

60 *Half Full,* sequence pastel for *Finding Nemo*
(Pixar Animation Studios, 2003)
Pastel on paper, 5 1/2 x 8 inches, 5 x 7 inches,
5 x 8 inches
Artwork provided by Pixar Animation Studio

61 *Roughs of colorscript,* for *WALL • E* (Pixar
Animation Studios and Walt Disney Pictures,
2008)
Ink and marker on paper, 17 x 13 3/4 inches
Artwork provided by Pixar Animation Studio

62 *Colorscript* for *WALL • E* (Pixar Animation Studios
and Walt Disney Pictures, 2008)
Digital painting, 13 1/2 x 30 inches
Artwork provided by Pixar Animation Studio

63 *WALL • E and EVE,* for *WALL • E* (Pixar Animation
Studios and Walt Disney Pictures, 2008)
Digital painting, 15 x 30 inches
Artwork provided by Pixar Animation Studio

64 *Ugly Al Following Maynard,* not dated
Oil pastel on paper, 9 x 14 1/2 inches
Courtesy of the artist

65 *Ugly Al Alone,* not dated
Oil pastel on paper, 8 3/4 x 13
Courtesy of the artist

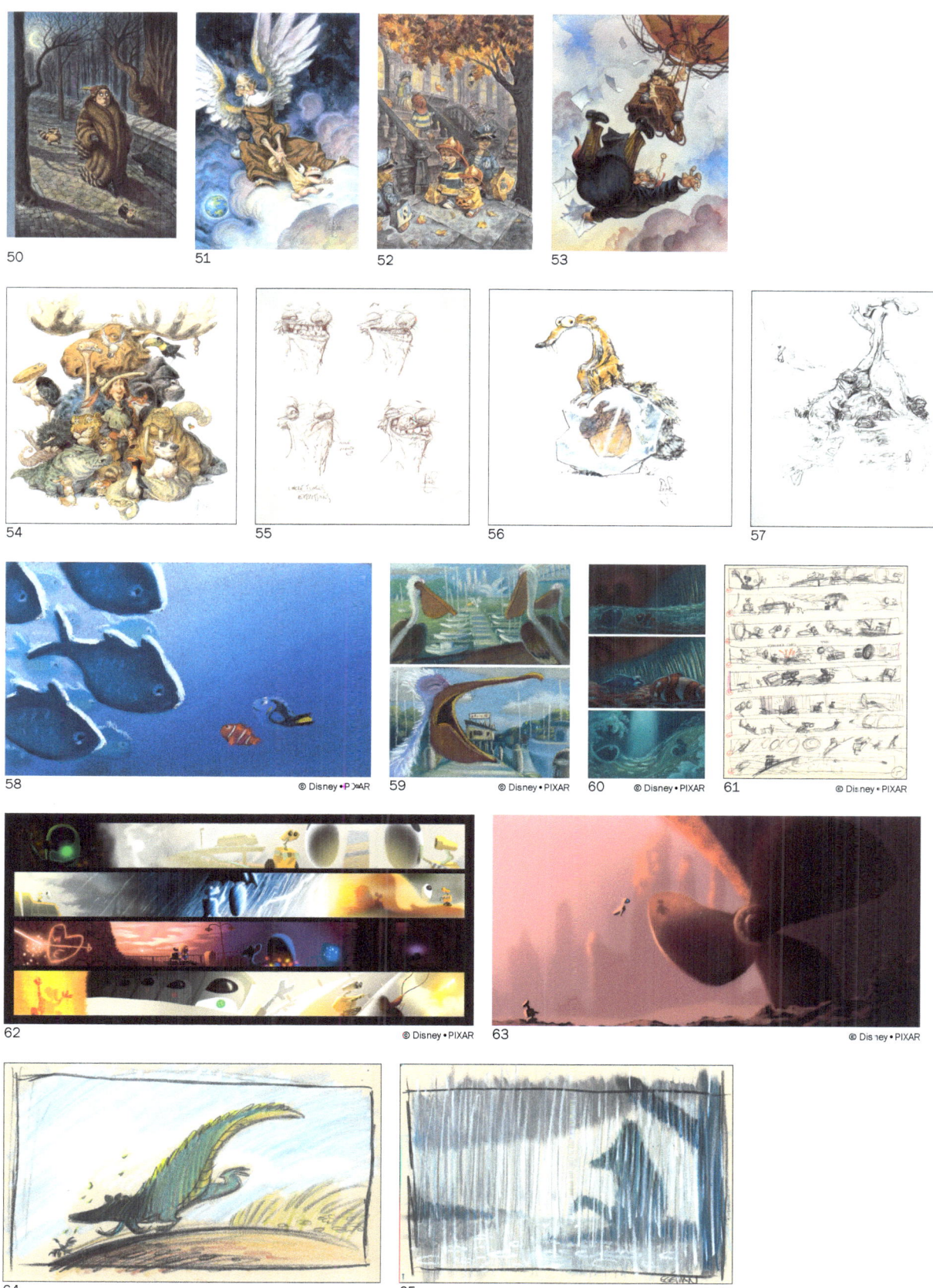

50

51

52

53

54

55

56

57

58

© Disney • PIXAR

59

© Disney • PIXAR

60

© Disney • PIXAR

61

© Disney • PIXAR

62

© Disney • PIXAR

63

© Disney • PIXAR

64

65

Unless otherwise indicated, photography by
Carson Zullinger. Additional acknowledgements
as follows, according to checklist number:

13: Photograph by Rick Echelmeyer

18 and 21: Images provided by National Portrait
Gallery, Smithsonian Institution

26: Image provided by lender

27, 30, 31, 34, 35, 36, 37, 38, 40, 41, 42, 43, 44,
45, 46, 47 48, 49, 51, 52, 53, and 54: Images
provided by artist

28, 29, 32, and 33: Photographs by Guy Patterson

58, 59, 60, 61, 62, 63, 64, and 65: Images provided
by Pixar Animation Studio